THOMAS J. HEAVEY

THE
CONTROL THEORY MANAGER

BOOKS BY WILLIAM GLASSER

The Control Theory Manager
The Quality School Teacher
The Quality School
Control Theory in the Classroom
Control Theory
Schools Without Failure
Reality Therapy
Positive Addiction
The Identity Society
Mental Health or Mental Illness?
Stations of the Mind

THE
CONTROL THEORY
MANAGER

Combining the Control Theory of
William Glasser with the Wisdom
of W. Edwards Deming to Explain
Both What Quality Is and What
Lead-Managers Do to Achieve It

William Glasser, M.D.

HarperBusiness
A Division of HarperCollins*Publishers*

HarperCollins books may be purchased for educational, business, or sales promotional use. For information please write: Special Markets Department, HarperCollins Publishers, Inc., 10 East 53rd Street, New York, NY 10022.

FIRST EDITION

Library of Congress Cataloging-in-Publication Data
Glasser, William, 1925–
    The control theory manager : combining the control theory of William Glasser with the wisdom of W. Edwards Deming to explain both what quality is and what lead-managers do to achieve it / by William Glasser. — 1st ed.
        p. cm.
    ISBN 0-88730-673-X
    1. Management. 2. Control theory. 3. Quality of products. I. Title
HD38.G565   1994
658.4'013—dc20   93-14546

94 95 96 97 98 ❖/RRD 10 9 8 7 6 5 4 3 2 1

To Naomi, my wife of forty-six years and the editor of my last six books, who died after a short bout with cancer in December of 1992. This is the first book in recent years that she had no part in editing but, as her imprint is on me, it is very much on this book. She was a good person, all who knew her loved her. Can more be said of anyone?

Acknowledgments

Unlike my previous books, this book I attempted to write alone. At the end, I recognized it needed a final polishing and I called one of my most skilled and trusted senior associates, Barbara Garner, for help. She came and worked with me for a full week. Her knowledge of control theory and her willingness to check every sentence for clarity has made this what I have been told by Hugh Van Dusen, my editor at Harper-Collins, is a very readable text. I thank her very much.

Contents

CONTENTS

Introduction

As this book is being written at the beginning of the Clinton administration, there are many positive economic signs being reported in the newspapers and on television. The stock market is at an all-time high and inflation seems well under control. All of this might indicate that my argument that we must move much faster and more completely to quality products and services may be overstated.

This, however, is not the case. Too many well-paid people are still being laid off. And what is far more significant is that the number of people employed by the private sector has also dropped significantly over the past ten years. Further, the government is drowning in red ink and only more good jobs in the private sector will stop this drain.

While the deficit seems to be an economic mystery and reputable economists say we need not worry about it, I don't think this argument will convince many people if taxes start going up and government cutbacks start to affect COLAs, health care, and jobs. For example, today's paper (*Los Angeles Times,* February 4, 1993) talked about shrinking the armed forces by 270,000 people who the economy will have to absorb or the government support. Many of these people will be minority members of our society who, although educated and skilled, will not easily find comparable jobs in their communities. This move has the potential to increase the unrest in the already restless centers of our large cities. And unrest is expensive.

From experience we can predict that, barring an economic catastrophe, spending will be hard to cut and taxes will be hard to raise. The only long-term solution is more people working in the private sector who, along with their employers, pay more taxes. To achieve this, *we have to buy the products we make,* not because we have raised tariffs to an exclusionary level but because our products are as good or better than those made elsewhere. I argue that only much better management of people will make this possible. If we look at our successful companies, we will find that they have taken managing for quality very seriously. *In doing this, they have discovered that they must focus on the workplace far more than on the work.* While what they have done should be a beacon for all companies—as Japan was a beacon for many of them—so far it has not worked this way. *This is because, without the control theory explained in this book, most managers find it almost impossible to con-ceptualize a quality workplace.* As long as we lack this vision, we will never achieve the level of quality we must achieve if we are to be competitive in an increasingly competitive world.

PART ONE

Managing for Quality

CHAPTER ONE

The Reason for This Book

Based on their common sense, almost all American managers are so convinced that they *"know"* why the people they manage behave the way they do that it never occurs to them that they could be wrong. This is why so many of them are puzzled. Managing workers with what they have "known" all their lives is not leading to *the quality work they know their companies need to achieve to be competitive.* That many companies are failing to achieve quality is painfully apparent. Their previous customers are buying what they believe are better foreign products, most of them made in Japan. More than any other reason, these products are better because foreign workers, especially Japanese workers, are managed much more effectively than we manage ours.

Led by Deming,[1] the Japanese have broken with common sense to embrace a management system, *lead-management,* that consistently produces quality. Americans continue to use boss-management, a traditional system that has always produced a lot of work and was quite competitive as long as everyone used it and no one's products were significantly better than anyone else's. In the next three chapters, I will describe both systems in detail.

But managers need more than a description; they need a clear understanding of why lead-management produces quality and boss-management does not. *Control theory, a new explanation of how we behave, supplies that understanding, and in this book I will strongly recommend that all managers learn to use this theory.* Workers who are managed by people who use control theory will consistently do quality work at a competitive cost. Part Two of this book will be devoted to a detailed explanation of this new theory.

It is only fair to warn readers that control theory is neither easy to accept nor to learn because we have to give up the common sense, stimulus-response (S-R), carrot-and-stick psychology that most of us have been using all our lives. We cling to this ancient psychology[2] even though some of its flaws are fairly obvious because, until the very recent introduction of control theory, there was nothing to replace it.

Control theory, in a form that is understandable and usable, has only been around since the early 1980s. Still, its acceptance is growing rapidly and my experience, as one of the leaders in teaching this theory, is that people who read what I write with an open mind find it to be so sensible and usable that many of them are already trying to give up bossing and start leading.

I also believe that the present stubborn, economic recession is a result of the significant improvement in the quality of the products that the Japanese, and others who have learned from Deming, have made available to consumers. After using these products for more than twenty years, almost everyone now wants—and even demands—quality; huge numbers of people have decided that it is not available in many domestic proucts.

This is new. Prior to what Japan has accomplished in the past quarter century, only the wealthy had access to quality products. The middle class, who make up the bulk of the world's consumers, could only see them in movies or glimpse them when the wealthy drove by. Now they can own them and the desire to accept nothing less has become contagious. In search of quality, billions of our dollars go overseas. Quality has now escaped from Pandora's box; shoddy is disappearing all over the world.

To achieve quality, lead-managers, using the concepts of control theory, embrace the following two procedures that rarely ever occur to boss-managers:

1. Learn what quality actually is, teach it to all who work in the organization, and then listen carefully to any worker who has an idea of how it may be further improved.

2. Manage everyone in the organization so that it is obvious to all workers that it is to their benefit to settle for nothing less than quality work.

This book focuses on managing people. It does not deal with nonhuman issues such as statistics, flow charts, finances or high technology. While these procedures are obviously essential to managing a successful business, companies are not failing because they lack this technical knowledge: *their failure is with people.* We seem unable to learn that workers will not do high-quality work much more because of the way boss-managers treat them than because they do not understand the technical or statistical aspects of what they are asked to do.

While this book is addressed to all managers, it is primarily directed to commercial managers who need to learn to manage workers so that what they produce can be sold for a profit. The amount of profit, however, will also depend on the company's ability to convince customers to buy. The surest way to do this is to produce quality products and to render quality service. Advertising is important, but no matter how convincing it may be, if it promises more quality than the product delivers, disappointed customers will stop buying and may never buy again. It is quality at a fair price far more than advertising that determines long-term profitability.

I, along with many others, accept that W. Edwards Deming is a pioneer in the field of managing workers so that they produce quality work at a competitive cost. I assume that readers are familiar with his basic ideas, so I restate them here only to support my thesis: a working knowledge of control theory is necessary if we are to significantly increase our practice of what Deming teaches. It is well known that his success has been mostly in

Japan, and that success has occurred because the Japanese have accepted his psychology even though he fails to explain it to the extent it is explained by control theory.

Deming talks extensively about the need to understand psychology and points out clearly that he believes human beings are *intrinsically,* rather than extrinsically, motivated. In doing so, he shows that he understands the basic premise of control theory. In my experience, we will not convince American managers to embrace Deming's ideas until we expose them to the complete theory of intrinsic motivation: control theory.

That American managers, even those who use Deming as a consultant, have been largely unable to duplicate the Japanese success is well documented in Andrea Gabor's 1990 book, *The Man Who Brought Quality to America.*[3] From Ms. Gabor's book, it is apparent that Deming's argument for intrinsic motivation is not strong enough to convince most American managers to stop bossing and to start leading.

Control theory supplies the convincing argument for lead-management that Deming does not provide. For example, in point eight of his fourteen points for management, Deming tells managers that in their dealings with workers they should "drive out fear." But as Ms. Gabor tells her story, it is clear that none of the three companies she writes about (Xerox, Ford, and General Motors) are willing to do this to the extent that Deming claims, and control theory explains, it must be done.

This is because the people at the top of these companies, much as those at the top of most American companies, believe that fear is an important motivator. They have believed this all their lives and they are not about to stop because an expert, even as successful an expert as Deming, tells them it is wrong. Control theory *explains clearly why workers who are not fearful do quality work.* And, the more they are treated in need-satisfying ways, the more willingly and joyfully they apply themselves, further increasing the quality of their work. More than most management consultants, Deming talks a lot about joy in work, but few bosses seem to hear this part of what he has to say.

What the Japanese did when they moved to lead-managing without knowing the underlying theory was unusual. It may have been because of their desperate effort to get their economy going after the destruction of World War II opened their minds to new ideas, but more likely it was because of their culture. They are much more willing than Americans to listen to people who they are told are experts, and Deming is one of the experts they were told to listen to.

I am not saying that this is always good or that our culture's lack of faith in experts is bad. All I am saying is that, in the case of Deming, this acceptance worked very well for them. He was introduced to them as an expert by officials in the MacArthur government and, because they revered MacArthur, they were willing to listen and to try what he suggested. What he advised them to do worked so well that they have continued to listen even if they still may not understand exactly why his advice works.

Unrealistic as it is, American business leaders, even when their companies are losing money or making much less than before, still tend to see themselves as "successful" managers. When their businesses fail to perform up to expectation, they blame unfair competition, poorly educated workers, the high cost of capital, excessive government regulation, overblown legal expenses, or demanding unions much more than their own inability to manage workers so that they do quality work at a competitive cost. They are confident that their "success" is related to their experience and common sense and have little faith in anyone who does not believe as they do.

As Ms. Gabor documents in her book, we pay lip service to people such as Deming much more than we pay attention to what they say, especially if they advise us to abandon common sense. It is unlikely we will embrace control theory until we have a clear idea of why we should take this step. In this book I will explain this new psychology in great detail. American managers who are willing to learn this theory—it helps a great deal if they also put it to work in their personal lives— will be able to lead-manage their workers so that they produce quality products and services at a competitive cost. When they do, "Buy American" will move from slogan to reality and our economy will get the real boost it needs. As long as we fail to achieve quality and continue to send billions of dollars overseas in search of it, our economy will limp along indefinitely.

CHAPTER TWO

Lead-Management Is the Basic Reform We Need

No management tradition is more firmly fixed in the United States than that of the boss. Bosses are in charge of the workers; they tell them what, when, and how to do their job. They have the power to reward them for doing a good job and to punish them for not doing what they are told to do. If workers have no union or civil service protection, not only their economic future but their happiness is in the boss's hands. Unfortunately, it is the unwise use of this power that effectively prevents us from achieving the quality work that is needed if we are to regain our competitive place in the market.

Workers don't trust bosses. If they are to expend both the mental and the physical effort necessary to achieve quality work, managers need to stop bossing and to do all they can to establish a trusting relationship with the workers. In this situation, trust means that the workers, based on experience, have come to believe that the manager has their best interests in mind. To establish this trust, the manager must learn to be warm, friendly, and supportive and to give up the traditional boss prerogatives of criticizing and coercing the workers. It is obvious that the kind of support recommended here does not come naturally or easily to bosses.

Therefore, what managers must do for quality is give up bossing or boss-management and start leading or using lead-management. Let me begin by explaining boss-management. It is not complicated. Reduced to its essentials it contains four elements:

1. The boss sets the task and the standards for what the workers are to do, usually without consulting the workers. Bosses do not compromise; the worker has to adjust to the job as the boss defines it or suffer any consequences the boss determines.

2. The boss usually tells, rather than shows, the workers how the work is to be done and rarely asks for their input as to how it might possibly be done better.

3. The boss, or someone the boss designates, inspects the work. Because the boss does not involve the workers in this evaluation, they do only enough to get by; they rarely even think of doing what is required for quality.

4. When workers resist, as they almost always do in a variety of ways, all of which compromise quality, the boss uses coercion (usually punishment) almost exclusively to try to make them do as they are told. In so doing, the boss creates a workplace in which the workers and the managers are adversaries. Bosses think that this adversarial situation is the way it should be.

It is obvious that boss-management is much more concerned with the agenda of the boss than the agenda of the workers. Because this is so obvious, many bosses have been able to see that boss-management is so adversarial that it is counterproductive. Because in industry we now have extensive research[1] to prove that boss-management is much less effective than lead-management, there is some softening of this hard-line approach in some high-tech and service industries where the educational and persuasive skills of the workers are paramount to the success of the company. Still, much more has to be done beyond softening the above description. *We have to get rid of bossing altogether and replace it with lead-managing or we will not succeed in producing the quality we need.*

Taken as a whole, the worst feature of boss-management is that it always results in the workers and the manager becoming adversaries. If this only occurred at the lowest level, it would be bad but not disastrous, since good design and engineering could make up for some of what the workers do not do. But, unfortunately, it occurs at every level, and when it does, there is little chance for quality. What happens is that, from bottom to top, each boss-manager is more concerned with his own point of view than anyone else's and this concern prevents the cooperation that quality work requires.

This does not mean that all boss-management is ineffective, but it is least effective where workers do not see the job as satisfying. It is most effective where workers and boss have similar agendas and where the

12

boss uses rewards more than punishment. But because it is not always ineffective does not in any way make it effective enough to consistently produce the quality we need.

As Deming says, "The goal is clear. The productivity of our systems must be increased. The key to change is the understanding of our managers and the people to whom they report about what it means to be a good manager." Deming goes on to say two more things that are always on the minds of lead-managers:

1. "A manager is responsible for consistency of purpose and continuity in the organization. The manager is solely responsible to see that there is a future for the workers." (No matter what a boss says, it is what he does that convinces or fails to convince the workers that he is concerned about their future.)

2. "The workers work in a system. The manager should work on the system to see that it produces the highest-quality product at the lowest possible cost. The distinction is crucial. They work in the system, the manager works on the system. No one else (only the manager) is responsible for the system as a whole and for improving it."

For workers to put the effort into the job that is necessary for quality work, they must be convinced that there is a future for them on the job. It is exactly the same as trying to convince a tenant to take good care of a rental property. If he believes that he can live where he is at a fair rent for as long as he wants, he will take far better care of the property than if he knows he will be evicted as soon as someone comes along who will pay a little more.

Lead-managers are open and aboveboard. They base their reputation on their intent to provide good pay for every employee as long as the company is making a reasonable return on its investment. They are willing to tell their employees in writing what a reasonable return is and what they can expect as their fair share of this return. Lead-managers are not shortsighted. They do not try to increase profits by cutting wages or reducing personnel, because they are aware that workers treated this way will reduce, not increase, the quality of their work. Lead-managers know it is low-quality work that leads to the wage cuts and layoffs that have reduced the profits.

To be specific, lead-management is defined by the following four statements that are parallel to the statements used to define boss-management:

1. Lead-managers engage the workers in an ongoing honest discussion of both the cost and the quality of the work that is needed for the company to be successful. They not only listen but they also encourage their workers to give them any input that will improve quality and lower costs.

2. The lead-manager (or someone designated by him or her) shows or models the job so that the worker who is to do the job can see exactly what the manager expects. The lead-manager works to increase the workers' sense of control over the work they do.

3. The lead-manager eliminates most inspectors and inspection. He or she teaches the workers to inspect

or to evaluate their own work for quality with the understanding that they know a great deal, almost always more than anyone else, about both what high-quality work is and how to produce it economically.

4. The lead-manager continually teaches the workers that the essence of quality is constant improvement. To help them, he makes it clear that he believes his main job is as a facilitator, which means he is doing all he can to provide them with the best tools and workplace as well as a friendly, noncoercive, nonadversarial atmosphere in which to work.

What is most difficult for boss-managers to realize is that it is *the system* itself that creates the problem. Their tendency is to blame the workers, but the fault is not with the workers—it is with the system. Deming used to agree with a colleague of his, Joseph Juran, who claimed that when a company fails to achieve quality the fault is 15 percent with the workers and 85 percent with the system created by the management. Deming now says the failure is 98 percent with the system and states categorically that only the management can change the system.

To be effective, most managers, even those who are trying hard to become lead-managers, must know a lot more than they know now about quality and what workers need to do to achieve it.

CHAPTER THREE

Explanations and Definitions

So far I have used the phrase "manage people for quality" a great deal but I have not really defined either management or quality. In this chapter I will define these terms as well as the other common terms that I use in this book. I will try to take nothing for granted so that there is no doubt in the reader's mind as to what I am saying. To begin, I will start with the most basic concept: quality.

QUALITY

I want to acknowledge that, if it were not for Deming, I would not have been nearly as aware of the importance of this concept as I am now. I give him full credit for this vital contribution. Deming and quality are synonymous. As much as all of us have always been aware of quality, it was Deming, more than anyone else, who pointed out how important it is that we keep this concept constantly in mind when we attempt to manage people. Managers must be aware of the fact that quality is at the core of what we all want all the time. Because this is what we all want, quality products and services, at an affordable price (not necessarily the lowest price), are the key to competing successfully in any commercial endeavor.

Quality is not definable if we are looking for a definition that everyone will agree upon. It is, however, easily definable in the sense that each of us always knows what it is for ourself. I will explain why this is so when I get to control theory in Part Two. Even without a precise definition, there is almost always a great deal of agreement among consumers as to what quality is. For example, if in 1992 the Ford Taurus was the best-selling car in America, we can be sure that a lot of people agreed it was a quality product. If your restaurant is prospering, it is very likely that you are providing quality food and service at a fair price. For the United States to prosper, we need both quality products and quality service; less will not do.

It is also safe to say that quality lasts; it is not faddish and it is always useful. Most school assignments lack quality because they are useless—a major cause of the nonquality education that permeates our schools. You can build a low-quality product that looks good and sells well for a while, but when people discover that it is not very useful, or it falls apart, they will stop buying it even if it is cheap. Deming further emphasizes that quality suffers if it remains the same. It can only be maintained through a continual effort to improve it, though generally the change will be slow. The only thing that continues to improve with time alone is an antique but so far no one has figured out how to make quality antiques.

As I will explain more precisely when I introduce control theory, once customers decide that something is quality, they rarely change their minds. People tend to be loyal to quality. It may take quite a while for cautious customers to decide what quality is, but once they make up their minds that a product or a service is quality, they will be reluctant to change that opinion. The product or the service has to be very bad for a long time before a loyal customer will give up on it.

Once the customer changes his mind and decides that a product is no longer quality, then it is very hard, maybe next to impossible, to get that person to change his mind back to where it was. Any business doing well through its ability to offer a quality product that wants to continue to prosper should have only one goal in mind: *continually improve the product and, at the same time, try to maintain or even lower the price.* Customers who realize that this is what the business is doing will be loyal through thick and thin.

THE FIVE CONDITIONS FOR QUALITY

Lead-managers understand that there are five basic conditions that have to be met if the workers they manage are to do quality work. From the standpoint of actually managing workers, however, it is not necessary for managers to keep all five in mind. If the lead-manager establishes the first four, the fifth condition will take care of itself. They are all based on control theory, they incorporate most of Deming's fourteen points, and, as you will soon see, they are not complicated. You may not agree with them, but you will have no difficulty understanding what they are.

The reason I reduced what managers need to keep in mind as they manage from the fourteen points Deming suggests to four of these five conditions is that most of us cannot keep more than three or four things in mind, especially as we attempt to do as difficult a job as managing people. Actually, as I explain the conditions, it will become apparent that the third and fourth conditions are so closely related that all you have to keep in mind is three, which should be easy. A word of caution, however: *I mean easy to keep in mind, not necessarily easy to put into practice.*

These conditions are:

1. The work environment must be warm and supportive. The workers must trust the managers. Although I have already mentioned this condition in the previous chapter, it is so important that I want to reaffirm it here. If workers are to do quality work, they must believe that the managers care about their welfare. Basically, what I am trying to explain is trust. I define **trust** as the belief that the person you trust not only will not hurt you but, at all times, has your welfare in mind.

Workers need to be assured that their jobs are safe,

that the company cares enough about them to treat them well and is willing to give them what they believe are not only fair wages but also a fair share of profits that have been earned through their quality labor. Above all, the managers must not attempt to coerce workers with threats of punishment or offers of rewards that are beyond the usual fair pay and fair share of the profits. Quality cannot be achieved when there is coercion or when there is antagonism between the workers and the managers or among the workers. Rewards that are not offered to all workers tend to divide them and create antagonisms highly destructive to quality.

Managers should do everything they can to encourage cooperation between manager and worker and among workers. Any and all problems related to production should be presented to the workers for suggested solutions. This should not be a token effort; it should be done in a way that the workers know that if they make a suggestion it will be listened to seriously. If what seems to be a good suggestion from the workers is not taken, the manager should make an effort to explain why. Workers who are treated in this way will produce far beyond what management expects. The limits of genuine manager-worker and worker-worker cooperation are barely tapped in boss-managed workplaces.

2. Since quality is always useful, workers should only be asked to do useful work and should be encouraged to contribute to the usefulness of what is being done. Managers should never ask workers to do anything that is not useful, which does not mean that the usefulness of what the worker is asked to do needs to be immediately apparent. However, it is the manager's responsibility to explain the job, so that in a reasonable amount of time the worker is able to see its usefulness. A lead-manager never says, "Don't bother me with questions; just do it." A lead-manager encourages a worker to question the usefulness of what she is asked to do and to give her opinion on how the work can be improved.

Nothing destroys quality more than asking workers to do things they do not believe are useful or refusing to listen to their ideas on how to make things better. When I was in the army, soldiers were punished by digging holes and then filling them in. To the extent that this goes on in business, it is always destructive to quality. In business, uselessness is more the result of thoughtlessness than the desire to punish and, in this sense, because workers asked to do useless work have done nothing wrong, it is even more destructive than in the army.

3. Workers are asked to do the best they can do. A basic assumption of quality is that it is the product of the best efforts of both the workers and the managers. If the previous conditions are in place, most workers will be more than willing to put out their best. Thus, as I have stated, this step is almost redundant. What assures that it will happen, however, is the implementation of the next, or fourth, condition.

4. From the time workers are hired, lead-managers will guide the process of helping them learn to continually evaluate their work. Then, based on this ongoing self-evaluation, lead-managers will encourage workers to improve the quality of what they do. For bosses, this will be the most difficult condition to implement. Bosses are so used to setting standards and then evaluating the worker's progress toward those standards that asking them to make this change is asking a great deal. But a worker's quality work is never the product of the evaluation of others, it is always the product of self-evaluation and continual improvement. The traditional "an inspector inspects, passes, or rejects the work" is static and does not involve the worker. It will lead to passable, even good work, but very little quality. Treated this way, workers will rarely, if ever, do what they are capable of doing.

The idea that quality is conformance to standards is only accurate if the workers themselves have a role in setting the standards and if they are encouraged to treat these standards as temporary in the sense that they can always be raised. The only reason to stop trying to improve is if to continue to try is no longer cost effective. Managers, however, should not jump quickly to the conclusion that an improvement is not cost effective. It may be highly cost effective in terms of increasing market share, because quality is the key to market share and market share is the key to long-term success.

Getting rid of the inspectors in a plant and letting the workers (with some training, mostly from each other) inspect their own work saves substantial money. Since it ensures that there will be constant improvement, it is almost the only way to quality. When workers and their work are evaluated by others, the stage is set for the workers to spend their time and energy evaluating the evaluators and trying to figure out how to do as little as they can. This is a distraction; it wastes time that could be spent on evaluating and improving what they do.

Deming strongly supports what I have just stated. In point 3 of his 14 points he says cease dependence on inspection to achieve quality. In point 12 he says eliminate annual ratings or merit system. But Deming has gone much further. In one of the most important statements that has ever been made he has stated: "No human being should ever evaluate another human being." If we would practice this recommendation, we would get rid of most of the destructive things we do to each other, because it is the distrust, antagonism, and anger that is almost always generated by being forced to submit to the evaluation of others that, more than anything else, blocks the road to quality.

5. Quality work always feels good. This is a nonoperational condition in that once a lead-manager puts the first four conditions into his management practices, there is nothing additional to do. If the workers then begin to do quality work, both they and the manager will feel good. In fact, assuming we do not use addicting drugs, we only feel good if we can introduce quality into our lives. As I will explain when I discuss control theory, the good feeling is neither the cause nor the result of the quality work. *It is what we feel when we do anything that gets us involved with quality.*

The good feeling, however, becomes a powerful incentive for workers to want to continue to do quality work so that they can experience the feeling again. And as quality becomes the norm, the manager will feel very good and have the incentive to continue to integrate the conditions of quality into her management. Why quality feels so good will become clear when I explain control theory in Part Two.

THE DEFINITION OF LEAD-MANAGEMENT

Lead-management is needed in many other situations besides business. In fact I first advocated it in my book, *The Quality School,*[1] where I applied it to how teachers are managed as well as to how they manage students. Obviously it is also needed in all other public jobs where the profit is the conservation of taxpayers' money. Although this book focuses on managing in industry and business, the five conditions of quality management apply in all instances. Therefore, lead-management can be accurately defined as the *skill to persuade*[2] workers (without using threats or coercion) to accept the manager's agenda, work hard at it, and do a quality job.

If you are a commercial manager, you will have to expand this definition to *the skill to manage the workers so that they produce a quality product or service at a*

24

cost low enough so that the company is assured a fair profit. Since all the people in the company are dependent for their livelihood on the company making a profit, quality work is the only way to assure long-run profitability.

In most cases, the workers in public agencies have no direct financial incentive to do quality work, for example, to ensure they will keep their jobs. But a look at the five conditions of quality shows that financial incentives are only *a part of the first condition;* they are not as important as we think. The psychological incentives such as trust and usefulness far outweigh the money as long as the money is seen as adequate. Deming says flatly, "Pay is not a motivator."

Very large companies are similar to public agencies in that high-level managers, even CEOs, may continue to draw large salaries while the company is losing huge sums of money. In the United States today, there is a substantial lag between the failure of top managers to manage effectively and their suffering any financial consequences for that failure. Boss-managed workers who are penalized by salary cuts or no raises and are threatened with layoffs become incensed when top managers get raises or huge salaries when the company is losing money. Angry workers will not do the quality work that is necessary if the company is again to become profitable.

At the time I was writing this book our automobile manufacturers were hemorrhaging money because they had still not convinced their former customers that they had sufficiently improved the quality of their cars. Now, nine months later, they are doing much better but their return to profitability is based more on cutting costs and a weaker dollar than on increased quality. Fortunately, they recognize this problem and are working hard to remedy it. For example, in one large automotive parts factory, we have been teaching control theory to a combined group of union leaders and managers and they are beginning to practice lead-management. The quality of the components they produce is very high and, based on this experience, it is my hope that more auto plants will embrace these ideas.

CHAPTER FOUR

The Ways We Relate to Each Other

There are four ways we relate to other people: (1) as friends, from casual to intimate; (2) as teacher to pupil; (3) as counselor to counselee; (4) as manager to worker. While I have so far limited my explanation of lead-managing to the manager-worker relationship, lead-managers must also learn to relate effectively as friends, teachers, and counselors. In this chapter, I will explain these three relationships, because I believe the more a manager is able to add them to his managing skills, the easier it becomes to manage.

FRIENDS: THE FIRST AND MOST COMMON WAY WE RELATE TO EACH OTHER

Friends are best defined as people who enjoy each other's company because they share interests. Certainly work is, for most adults, the most common interest they share with others. It is almost impossible to meet another human being and not ask, and be asked, "What do you do?" Most adults make many of their friends through work.

While managers have often been instructed not to become friends with workers because workers may take advantage of this friendship, most managers have found that if they are friendly, it is easier to persuade workers to work hard and do a good job. Lead-managers find that as long as they take a friendly interest in what the workers are doing, asking them to do only useful work and to evaluate what they do, workers will not take advantage of their friendship. They will work much harder than if the manager is aloof or unfriendly.

Managers must be aware that friends will do more for each other than strangers. Thus, it is important not to ask so much that the worker believes the manager is taking advantage of the friendship. The best approach is to discuss the situation and ask for input. For example, the manager might say, "We have got to do all this work before we quit for the day. How do you suggest we go about it?" What this illustrates is that *how* you ask friends to work hard is often more important than *what* it is you ask them to do. People are capable of doing prodigious amounts of work if they believe their knowledge and skills are appreciated and they are involved in making decisions about their work. Making demands will rarely produce much work and it will never produce quality work.

If there were an axiom to friendship it would be, "The better we know someone and the more we like what we know, the more we want to do, even enjoy doing, for that person." Acting on this axiom, lead-managers would reveal much more about themselves than managers usually do. What follows is a list of what I recommend you might do to accomplish this. I realize the list is specific, but suggestions have to be specific or they are meaningless.

Also, *take your time;* do only as much as you are comfortable with. The reason to go slowly is that if you try too hard or go too fast, the people you manage may interpret what you are doing as overselling and may doubt your sincerity. Because they are not used to this "let's get to know each other approach," they may interpret too much effort on your part as coercive and you will be less effective. It is also best if you integrate these suggestions into the ordinary routine of your work. Occasions will arise when covering this or that point on the list will be natural and easy and you should take advantage of these opportunities.

What I recommend may seem excessive. Partly this may be because very few people who have managed you have ever done anything close to what I am suggesting here. But some have, and I believe that these are the managers you worked the hardest for and whom you still remember fondly. This certainly was the case for me. If you take your time, you will find that these suggestions are very enjoyable to implement and, in a quality workplace, it is very important that you enjoy the people you work with. As your people get to know you, they will, in turn, reveal more and more about themselves. You and they will gain much of the closeness that is needed if you are to satisfy the first condition of quality—a warm and friendly workplace.

When a natural opportunity arises, share the following with the people you manage:

1. Who you are.
2. What you stand for.
3. What you will ask the workers to do.
4. What you will not ask them to do.
5. What you will do for them or with them.
6. What you will not do for them.

Let me now go through this list item by item and explain why each point is important. Do not, however, restrict yourself to this list. Add anything you believe will increase what you and your workers know and like about each other.

Who You Are

Because we need people so much if we are to satisfy our needs, we are all very curious about people. One thing we like so much about television is that we get to see and hear people in ways that would otherwise be impossible and, if someone we know is on, we make an extra effort to see that program. For example, suppose your CEO were scheduled to be on television. Wouldn't you make an effort to hear what she had to say? Further, suppose she revealed something about her life that you did not suspect, that as a twenty-year-old she had been a turned-on, tuned-out hippie. Then she explained why she decided to change her life.

Even if you did not work directly under her, if you liked what she said, wouldn't your relationship with her and with the company change to some extent—most likely for the better? Might you not respect the CEO a little more for having overcome early adversity? Wouldn't you listen to her more attentively when she dealt with company problems that affected you? Wouldn't she become a little more human to you than before? Sophisticated as you may be, you would still appreciate learning things you didn't know about a person as important to you as she is.

Most of us tend to know very little about people except those we live with. While you are very important to those you manage, as a human being, you may be a complete mystery. Not knowing the facts, they fantasize and may build a false image of you based on very little real knowledge. As dull as these may be to you, people are interested in mundane statistics such as your age; your marital status; whether or not you have children and, if so, their ages; whether you have a mother, father, or grandparent in your life; whether you live in a house or apartment; what kind of car do you drive. Even more, they want to know about your interests: what have you done besides what you are doing now? what are your favorite television programs? what music do you listen to? what food do you like best? what things do you dislike? The list could go on and on, but if you do not make your stories too long, they will be quite interested in what seems so unimportant to you.

What You Stand For

Most interesting to all of us, and usually totally unknown to most of the people you manage, is what you stand for. Do you attempt to practice what you preach and is it difficult for you? Do you have a stand on what's going on in the world, for example, on the riots in our cities, and what would you do about them if you had the opportunity? Do you vote and what do you do to get to know the candidates and issues? The list could go on, but what you stand for and why you stand for it is of endless interest to those who work with you.

If the people you manage respect you—and respect is built out of satisfying knowledge as well as good treatment—you can have a positive effect on them. You may help them form opinions that will be supportive of the work they are doing, for example, why making the effort to treat a difficult customer well will pay off in the long run. In some instances, you may be the first person of your status whom they have ever known much about. Not knowing people like you, they may form their opinions with insufficient information or information from biased or uninformed people. To help them form more accurate opinions, they need to find out what you think about and why.

Finally, if I were you I would explain to the people you manage, and reexplain as the situation arises, *that you believe no one should put another person down.* Explain that most of the trouble and friction among people is caused by putting others down. Organizations are filled with cliques and groups based on power, or lack of it, that cause endless friction and make it impossible for quality work to flourish. Quality is achieved through harmony and respect; there is no other way.

What You Will Ask Them to Do

In a quality organization, you should make sure workers know what you will ask them to do: never surprise them. Telling them what you will ask them to do is meaningless if you don't, yourself, do as you ask them to do. For example, if you ask them to be on time and ready to go to work, then you must be on time and ready to go to work. If you tell them that this is the rule from now on, then it must be the rule: no exceptions for the people who have the power.

In a quality organization, although you will not punish or put anyone down, you should tell workers this does not mean you will not handle problems. Tell them you arc going to ask them to work with you to solve any problem that arises no matter how small. You will ask them to do this as individuals, in small groups, or even in large groups if there is a big problem that is affecting almost everyone. You are also much more interested in their solving their own problems than in your doing it for them. You should encourage them to get together without you and then to discuss the results with you.

What You Will Not Ask Them to Do

Considering that most of your workers will come from boss-managed organizations, explain that in a quality organization you will no longer ask them to be subservient or to do things just because you say so. You want them to speak up and suggest how to do a job better, not to keep quiet. Also explain that you are not going to ask them to do anything useless and, if they think a certain practice or procedure is useless, they should be sure to discuss it with you.

What You Will Do for Them or with Them

In a quality workplace they will want to make an effort to learn and improve, so you will make it clear to them that you are available to help them in any way you can or, if possible, in any way they want. You are their friend, you are always on their side, and it will never be you against them. For example, if they need more time to figure something out or to do a better job, you will give it to them, advise them on where to get help, or take off your coat, roll up your sleeves, and pitch in. If they have questions, you will either answer them or find someone who can. If they have an idea about how to make things better, you will take the time to listen to them. They are doing the work; you are doing all you can to support them.

At the same time, tell your workers you are not perfect and, if they find that you are not doing as you say, they should not be afraid to tell you and you will explain or try to change. Also tell them that when problems arise on the job, you are going to ask them for help and you welcome their ideas. Show them you value their help by getting together with a small group of workers and asking them to brainstorm as a group. This shows that you believe in cooperation and it encourages them to work together to solve problems and, in some cases, to solve them without even telling you what they are.

What You Will Not Do for Them

You will not do their work or solve the problems they should solve themselves. You will not tell them what to do unless it is obvious that they need direct help. Mostly, you will tell them that quality comes from their figuring it out, not from being told what to do. You communicate that you are their leader, not their boss. More and more you will stop evaluating their work and turn this job over to them. If they ask you for your opinion, you will give it, but not unless they are also willing to express their opinions and defend them. Explain that to be successful in life, we must evaluate ourselves and work to improve: we cannot and should not depend on others to do this for us.

LEAD-MANAGERS AVOID THE THREE THINGS THAT DESTROY FRIENDSHIP

The three things that people commonly do that are always destructive to friendship are:
1. Criticizing the friend's behavior.
2. Asking too much of the friend.

3. Attempting to coerce the friend to do what the friend does not want to do.

Even strong relationships like marriages, family ties, lifelong friendships, and business partnerships may founder when one of the friends starts to use one or more of these destructive behaviors. Later, as I explain the control theory that underlies this whole book, I will explain clearly why this is so. Even before I do this I have a hunch that most readers will tend to agree with these three basic destroyers of friendship.

If very close friendships can be shattered by one or more of these destructive behaviors, it is obvious the more fragile friendships that exist between managers and workers are far more easily destroyed by the same behaviors. And of the three, criticism, even if the manager believes it is justified or constructive, is probably the most destructive. Coercion, which means threatening or trying to bribe, is almost as bad. Asking too much, as long as criticism or coercion is not added to it, is rarely, by itself, destructive of friendship. The first thing that a successful manager learns is not to criticize or coerce. If this is all the manager learns, it is still a huge amount. Just refraining from criticizing or coercing will greatly increase your effectiveness as a lead-manager.

COUNSELOR TO COUNSELEE: THE SECOND WAY WE RELATE

Counseling is best defined as one person, the counselor, helping another person, the counselee, *who wants the help.* The help is usually in the form of giving advice or making suggestions. On the other hand, if you are dealing with a person who is obviously not doing well but *does not want help,* that person cannot be counseled. This does not mean that he can't be helped, but it is much more accurate to refer to the help as managing rather than counseling.

For example, you would *counsel* a worker who came to you and asked for advice on how to deal with a work problem or a personal problem. You would also counsel a worker who asked you how to cope with another worker who was not cooperating in getting the work done. *Managing* would be the situation in which you recognized that a worker was doing badly at work but refused your initial offer to discuss the situation with him. A typical example of this would be when all signs point to the fact that a worker is drinking to the point where it is obviously interfering with his work. It could also be when a worker asked you to approach another worker and try to get him to see that what he is doing is interfering with the quality of the work.

What I will focus on here is how to counsel workers who want help. Later in the book, I will explain how to approach workers who do not want help. Problems like these are very common and lead to great expense for the company, and a manager who is capable of handling them is a valuable asset. This aspect of managing is much more difficult than counseling and I will wait to explain it until after I have explained control theory, because understanding this theory is vital to learning this procedure.

Managers will frequently be called upon to counsel, because workers or subordinates naturally look to their superior or supervisor for advice and guidance in areas that have nothing to do with the job. In the case of lead-managers, whom they trust, this could be frequent, and the willingness to offer brief, friendly counseling should be routine.

A variation of counseling that a lead-manager should use frequently is to ask a worker for help with any sort of a problem the manager notices. Deming claims that the worker who does the job knows more about it than anyone else, and there is no better way to tap this expertise than to ask the worker for advice on some aspect of what he knows and then, in almost all cases, take his advice.

Workers who find out that their manager depends on them for advice will work very hard with few complaints. The key is to ask for the advice and then try very hard to take it. If it cannot be used as given, you should use as much as you can and thank the worker for what he suggested. If possible, also explain to the worker why only some of the advice was usable, and from this honest discussion the worker can learn more about the broader implications of the job. Keep in mind that when a worker learns that any of his advice was useful, that knowledge will spur him to work harder and quality will increase.

Managers should try to get close to individual workers who are especially liked and respected by their fellow workers. These workers can then be approached by the manager to feel out another worker who is having a problem and to offer help or advice without the manager's direct intervention. If, however, the problem worker asks the helping worker, "Did the manager ask you to do this?," the helping worker should always tell the truth by revealing, "The manager thought a little help was needed and asked me to talk with you. If you want to find out more about what is going on, ask him directly. He has no reason to keep this secret."

Managers, especially, should develop some counseling skills in the area of personal finances as workers who are in financial hot water are often distracted and the quality of their work suffers. Nothing hampers workers' efforts or tests their honesty more than financial troubles, and a good manager should learn to be a good financial advisor. Managers should always anticipate difficulties and deal with them before they get serious; nowhere is this more needed than with finances. Quality is directly related to loyalty, and when workers are involved in giving and getting advice to and from managers whom they consider to be their friends, they tend to be extremely loyal.

In union shops, managers need to develop a great sensitivity to the relationships between themselves, the union leaders, and the workers. A person can be a union member and still be on friendly terms with the manager. What is important is that the manager does not take advantage of that friendship and counsel a worker in a way that the manager's advice puts the worker into conflict with the union.

The danger of giving advice is that it could be destructive to the friendship you are always trying to establish. Even when the worker asks for advice, you should be careful not to criticize him if he does not take your counsel—and certainly, there should be no coercion to take the advice either. If this occurs, the distrust of the worker will be much more destructive than if the advice were not offered at all. People who ask for help will often refuse good counsel, and managers should be prepared to accept this fact of life.

TEACHER AND PUPIL: THE THIRD WAY WE RELATE

For a commercial organization to achieve quality, it must function as a school, but this school must be far different from the schools that most workers attended. In public school, the students try to get through far more than they try to learn, because most of what they are asked to learn has little or no use in their lives. The diploma, however, is usually quite useful. In the company school, the usefulness of everything workers are asked to learn should be either obvious or fully explained by whomever is teaching. In this school, the managers, themselves, must be prepared to teach but, even more, they must train skilled workers to teach needed skills to other workers.

All this education is needed because quality is not a static thing. Quality is the result of constantly improving the system, and the only way to do this is to learn better ways to do the job. As Deming says in point 13, "Institute a vigorous program of education and self-improvement for everybody." Workers must be encouraged to be constantly on the alert for better ways to do their job and to report to the manager when they think they have discovered something worthwhile. Lead-managers give workers who make discoveries their attention and immediately start planning how these improvements can be taught to all who could use them. If managers are not prepared to listen, the workers will not talk with them and are even likely to stop trying to improve what they are doing. Thus, a good teacher listens to her pupils, and only then can she be assured that they will listen to her.

In almost all instances, both the managers and workers will be products of schools that not only taught useless material but few teachers in these schools listened to the pupils. They also attended schools where teachers used criticism and coercion to "motivate" students and where only a handful of students worked hard and did quality work. In a quality organization, this must be completely changed. All the work must be quality work and all the workers must be taught to be quality workers, which also means to be quality teachers and learners.

Unlike school, where students are tested mostly on what they can remember (almost all of which is quickly forgotten), only what is relevant to doing quality work should be taught on the job. The only test of what is learned is *can the learner apply it successfully to the job.* Success is measured by the single criterion: Does it improve the quality of the work? In a lead-managed operation, it would be the worker's evaluation of his own work that would determine whether the education led to improving the quality of the product or the service. Everything that is taught should be carefully explained, so that all the workers clearly understand that what they are learning relates to improving the quality of the work and the workplace.

To function as a school, the organization needs to adopt a definition of education that is far different from how education was defined in the schools that both the managers and the workers attended. In almost all schools, and even in a great many colleges, education is defined as *learn, usually memorize, what the teacher teaches or face the consequences of low grades or failure.* To get credit, students have to pass the test, but passing the test almost never indicates that what was learned had anything to do with usefulness or quality. That is why our schools are so low in quality, because students, coerced to learn what has little use in the real world, only do enough work to get by.

In a quality organization, education would be defined as it should be defined in our schools: *it is the process through which the workers (as students) discover that learning adds quality to their lives.* For a commercial organization, this definition would be extended to *adding quality to the workers' lives and also to the lives of the customers.* Education would then become student centered and, in the case of commercial organizations, also customer centered. Managers who accept their role as teachers and who are willing to define education as it is defined here are vitally needed if we are to have quality organizations that can survive in today's highly competitive, commercial world.

SUMMARY

In the first four chapters of this book, I have covered the aspects of management that need to be examined before I explain control theory. I have defined lead-management, quality, and the five conditions that a lead-manager must put into place if he is to achieve the quality we need. I have also described the three additional relationships—friendship, counseling, and teaching—that a manager must add to his skills if he is to be successful. I have focused on the specific change that we have to make—from bossing to leading—if we are to increase the productivity and the quality of the work we do. I am now ready to turn to the explanation of control theory, because I believe this theory provides much of what Deming calls "the profound knowledge" that is needed if we are to make the move to quality.

PART TWO

Control Theory

CHAPTER FIVE

All We Do Is Behave and All Significant Behavior Is Chosen

Most of us don't think much about behavior, but if we did we would realize that all any human being does from birth to death is behave. What most of us would not realize even if we thought about it is that almost all this behavior, in fact all of it that has even the remotest effect on our lives, is chosen. For example, when we manage people, we *choose what we do* and the workers we manage *choose what they do*. Therefore, our ability to succeed in managing, as well as anything we attempt, depends on how well we learn to choose effective behaviors.

Bosses choose boss-management, but it is not an effective behavior because few bossed workers will choose to make quality products or perform quality services. The Japanese, taught by Deming and others, are embracing what is obviously lead-management even though they do not use this term to describe what they do. In doing so, they are persuading the workers to choose the behaviors that lead to the quality products that consumers have always wanted and, having recently experienced them, now demand.

In competitive industries, managers who are not willing to learn to lead will preside over the destruction of their companies. Many American companies realize the importance of quality and are trying to follow Deming, but most have not succeeded because their boss-managers are unwilling to give up bossing. As stated, this is because, following their common sense, they believe in a psychology that tells them bossing is correct.

To review briefly, boss-managers, like almost all human beings, believe in and manage according to the traditional theory of human behavior: stimulus-response (S-R) psychology. They follow it mostly because it supports their common-sense belief that people can be made, through reward or punishment, to do what the manager wants them to do whether they like it or not. And, to some extent, they follow it because no one has ever offered them another theory. They have nothing to turn to if they suspect, as I am sure many do, that what they believe may be wrong. Therefore, it is not that they believe in S-R theory so absolutely that they cannot change. It is more that, for almost all people, stimulus-response theory is all there is.

Control theory, as it is applied to human behavior, is very new. Although it was described as early as 1973,[1] it was first presented in a form that people could use both in their work and in their life in my 1984 book, *Control*

Theory.[2] It is so new that even Deming, whose teachings about how to manage people follow it closely, does not teach it. Deming's practice preceded the control theory that I believe supports it, actually a very common situation. For example, Columbus, and many who followed him, sailed as if the world were round long before this was actually proved. Control theory is so new that it has not yet been proved. Those who accept it do so because it makes more sense than stimulus-response theory and, when applied to management, it works. For example, workers who are managed by lead-managers who follow control theory do quality work, *whether they realize they are following it or not.*

However, and this is the thrust of this book, once managers learn and begin to use control theory, there is a good chance that they will give up bossing and choose to become lead-managers. They make this choice because they have learned people function as control systems and, with this knowledge, they are able to make constant improvement in the way they manage. It is the same with sailors. Those who knew the world was round navigated much better than those who sailed as if it was round but did not actually know it.

We believe that managers should learn and use control theory with all the people they manage. To follow up on this belief, I will explain it in this part of the book. I also practice what I preach in my own organization, which I believe has become large and successful because, using lead-management exclusively, we are constantly improving all we do.

If you want to teach managers to become lead-managers, you should begin by explaining control theory to them, so that they understand why lead-managing works. Then practice it as you work with them. If the managers you are teaching begin to stop threatening and coercing, you can see that they are on the right track. You cannot, however, put lead-managing into a company, because this would be bossing and leading cannot come from bossing. This is confirmed by a basic tenet of control theory: *You cannot make anyone do what he or she does not want to do. You can only teach him a better way and encourage him to try it. If it works, there is a good chance he will continue.*

Many companies are in the process of "installing" Deming or TQM,[3] but they are putting it in by edict instead of by teaching and demonstrating and, as stated, this is a contradiction of the ideas themselves. Further, attempting to install it without teaching the control theory that explains it is unlikely to work. People cannot practice something as new as quality management without understanding the theory that explains it. As Deming says, "Knowledge is prediction and knowledge comes from theory. Experience teaches nothing without theory. Do not try to copy someone else's success. Unless you understand the theory behind it, trying to copy it can lead to complete chaos."[4]

Until they are taught differently, most managers will continue to believe that you can make people do what they don't want to do. This disparity—control theory claims you cannot make people do what they do not want to do and stimulus-response theory claims you can—is the fundamental difference between the two theories. As practiced by almost all people, stimulus-response theory is based on the belief that human behavior is caused by a stimulus, which is an event or a situation that is *outside the behaving person.*

For example, most people, including all boss-managers, follow the popular, common-sense S-R psychology and believe we answer a telephone because it rings or stop our car because a traffic light turns red. Control theory is just the opposite. It is based on the premise that all human behavior is caused by *what goes on inside the heads of each behaving human being.* It stands in sharp contrast to common sense as it goes on to state that what happens outside of us *does not cause us to do anything.*

Therefore, we do not answer a phone because it rings, stop our car because a traffic light turns red, or do anything else that we do because of what happens outside of us. We are well aware that many times we choose not to answer a ringing phone and that, in an emergency, we will run a red light. Control theory claims that when we choose to answer a phone, and do *all* else we choose to do, *it is because this chosen behavior satisfies one or more of five basic needs that are built into the genetic structure of our brain.*

Therefore, if we do not choose to answer a ringing phone or do not choose to do the quality work that a manager is trying to persuade all workers to choose, it is because, at this time, neither answering the phone nor doing the quality work is satisfying enough to one or more of five basic needs. We do not always do what is expected of us. If it does not sufficiently satisfy one or more of our basic needs, we won't choose to do it.

What is called a *stimulus* in stimulus-response theory is, in control theory, more accurately called *information,* and we all know that, by itself, *information does not make us do anything.* It tells us what is going on, but it is still up to us to figure out what to do that is best for us. Control theory explains that what is best for us is always what we believe is most satisfying to one or more of five genetic needs built into our brain.

This leads us to the basic difference between boss and lead-manager. The boss-manager thinks that he can stimulate the worker into doing what he wants, usually through threats or punishment, regardless of whether these are satisfying to the workers' needs. The lead-manager knows that all he (or anyone else) can do is to give the workers information. Based on that information, it will be up to the workers to figure out if they should do the quality work that is needed if the company is to succeed.

To do this, lead-managers try to give workers information that will persuade them to come to the conclusion that *expending the effort to do quality work will satisfy them better than anything else they can do at this time.* Unless they are taught, workers won't know about needs or control theory but, since these needs are built into their genetic structure, they must act as if they do. For lead-managers, however, *this information is vital.*

You cannot give a worker need-satisfying information unless you know what the needs are.

THE FIVE BASIC HUMAN NEEDS

At conception, when the egg and sperm join to make the single cell that will eventually subdivide the billions of times it takes to create a baby, what guides this process are the 100,000 genes that are present in that first cell and copied into all subsequent cells. It is well known that the genes are the instructions for what each individual is to become physically. All of us are aware of the fact that the genes lead to the color of our eyes, the shape of our nose, and all else *that will make up our physical structure and the physiology that makes it function.* Scientists believe that it takes considerably less than the full 100,000 genes to do this structural task, which leaves the function of many genes unaccounted for.

What I postulate is that some of these "excess" genes have nothing to do with our structure or physiology; *they are the basic or underlying cause of all of our behavior.* For example, from birth to death, almost all of us who are genetically normal live our lives in certain recognizable ways, and we do this because our brains, driven by these behavioral genes, are constantly telling us what to try to do. This genetic motivation can be summarized into what I call *the five basic needs.*

Together these needs, in a myriad of ways that each of us figures out, cause us to search for sufficient (1) *survival;* (2) *love and belonging;* (3) *power or recogni-*

tion; (4) *freedom;* (5) *fun.* Unless we are born genetically flawed, which means we do not seem to need what genetically normal people need, we tend to be more similar than different in how much we believe we have to do to satisfy each of these five basic needs. Such a flaw was illustrated by the character Dustin Hoffman played in the film *Rainman,* who did not have anywhere near the normal need for love and belonging.

Survival: The First Basic Need

From the standpoint of evolution, survival probably came first and it makes sense to list this need first. Certainly we can feel the push of this need whenever we are hungry, thirsty, cold, or tired. We also feel its impact sexually, because driven by hormones derived from this need we struggle for sex so that the species will survive. I realize that in humans there are other genetic motivations for sex such as love, power, and fun so, because it is driven by at least four of the five needs, the human sex drive is strong and longlasting. There is no reason to discuss this obvious need further except to say that it must have come first and that all the other needs were probably derived from it. By now, as I will explain shortly, they have become separated from survival and stand alone.

Love and Belonging: The Second Basic Need

All humans, and to a lesser extent many higher animals such as apes and wolves, need to feel loved.

Friendship, or a sense of belonging with others, is also a vital part of this need. Probably it derived from survival as human infants need so much care that love evolved as a strong separate need to make sure that they get this care. Many parents are willing to make sacrifices to save the life of a child. The more a manager can foster a sense of friendship and belonging in the workplace, the higher the quality of the work. Workers who do not believe that anyone cares about them personally tend to work only for survival, which is hardly a motivation for quality work.

Power: The Third Basic Need

Among higher animals, humans have by far the greatest need for power. This need becomes most obvious in boss-managed workplaces where coercing people is not only accepted, it is the thing to do. Unfortunately, as bosses coerce, quality suffers. For most of us who do not have or want the opportunity to boss, this need is well satisfied if we believe people will listen to us and maybe act positively on what we have to say, which is the basis of lead-management. In the sense that workers are asked for their input, given useful work, and encouraged to evaluate what they do—the conditions for quality—this need will be well satisfied in lead-managed workplaces.

Freedom: The Fourth Basic Need

We live in a reasonably free society and political leaders extol the virtues of freedom every chance they get. But talking about it and practicing it are two very different things, and most workplaces are dominated by "he who pays the piper calls the tune." In the beginning, freedom was a requisite for successful survival, but it soon became a separate need. No one reading this book would seriously deny that, as they struggle in what are mostly boss-managed workplaces, freedom is on their mind much of the time. As explained, lead-management is democratic. To the extent that we can manage people in a way that they believe they have some freedom to express themselves (and be listened to), quality will increase. Workers who are dominated will spend too much of their energy struggling to gain a sense of freedom, which is energy that could be better spent in the pursuit of quality.

Fun: The Fifth Basic Need

We are the only creature who laughs and probably the only creature who consciously seeks fun. Between travel and entertainment, perhaps more money is spent in the search for fun than any of the other needs. But fun is more than just trying to relax and enjoy oneself. Fun is a basic need because it is the genetic reward for learning and, more than anything, we travel to learn. We are born knowing less than all other higher animals, and we have to learn the most in order to satisfy our needs. Evolution, which does not leave much to chance, has provided fun as an incentive to learn.

What is most fun is when we learn something that is obviously need satisfying, for example, children squeal with laughter when they first walk. The more a manager can combine learning and laughter into the process of teaching workers how to improve what they do, the more quality will be achieved. When management is grim and domineering, little quality will come from that workplace.

Although there are differences in what will satisfy us—*Rainman* is an example of such a difference—most people want similar amounts of love, power, fun, freedom, and the means to survive. *Similar,* at least, in the sense that all human traits, both physical and psychological, follow a normal, statistical distribution. For example, while there are no adults taller than nine feet or shorter than one foot, the vast majority of us are between five and six feet tall. And although a few people will give up and die when times get hard, most of us will struggle very hard to survive. Still it would be foolish not to be aware that there are differences in the strengths of the needs—that is, it would be unwise to hire a person for the lonely job of night watchperson who had an obvious strong need for love and belonging.

Of the five needs, four are psychological. Only the need for survival is physiological in that we think of survival as the need for food, water, and shelter. In this book we will concentrate on the psychological needs—*love, power, freedom, and fun*—as it is the satisfaction of these needs at work far more than the need to survive that leads a worker to do quality work. This does not mean that many workers do not think of their job as a means to survive but, even if this is true, few workers will do quality work based on satisfying this need alone. If survival is all they believe the job provides, they will rarely do more than is required to keep their jobs.

If we want quality, we have to structure ʰ that it will satisfy much more than ⁿⁿ ple, people managing workᵉ such as in civ¹ ᵉᵉʳᵛⁱᶜᵉ fits if they wₐ they come to ment worker so that workers experience tᵢₑₛₑ ₚₛ ... has been summarized under the conditions for quality in Chapter 3.

No one can satisfy another person's needs. We all must do this for ourselves. What we, as lead-managers, can offer is what we believe is the opportunity; it is up to the worker to agree that this is indeed a need-satisfying opportunity and to take advantage of it. For example, we can get our workers together and explain to them what we want done and ask them to come up with the way to achieve it. When they make suggestions, we can listen to them, help them try the ideas, and encourage them to evaluate what they are now doing and to continue doing it if it is better than what they did before. Most workers find that their needs for belonging and power are satisfied by this approach, and it is these needs that seem to be the hardest to satisfy at work.

What makes this approach satisfying is quite specific: workers managed this way believe they have more *control* over what they are doing than if they are bossed, and it is this control that leads us to the core of control theory: *We all want to have a sense of control over what we choose to do. This is why control theory is called control theory.* Since we have no choice but to try to satisfy our needs, and since we have to behave to do this, the more we believe we are in effective control of our own behavior, the better we will be able to carry out the instructions of our genes.

This means that we are in control of our lives when we are able to satisfy our needs and, since the more we satisfy them the more we are in effective control, we are always trying to improve how we do this. Although Deming does not teach control theory, he is saying the same thing when he says that we are always trying to increase the quality of our lives. However, he does not define quality as specifically as it can be defined by control theory: quality is anything we do or learn that is highly satisfying to one or more of our basic needs.

When people try to force us to do what we do not want to do (because we do not find it need satisfying), we feel out of control or, more accurately, that we are losing control. What we may also feel is that our lives are losing quality. Similarly, when we are forced by lack of money to buy a low-quality product or suffer poor service, we feel as if we are losing control. Or if we have plenty of money but a quality product or service is not available, it is likely that we will feel the same lack of control and, as I will explain shortly, all pain is the result of our not being able to satisfy our needs to the extent that we want to satisfy them.

Therefore, satisfying all of our needs, psychological as well as physiological, is the purpose of our lives. We can no more deny the importance of our psychological needs than we can deny that to survive we must breathe. Gaining love, power, fun, and freedom is not usually as urgent as breathing, but these needs can never be ignored for very long; it will hurt too much. Suicide, a tragic but, unfortunately, too-common behavioral choice, is almost always contemplated or carried out when a person has lost a lot of love, power, or freedom. A person may also kill himself when he is faced with starvation or freezing, but that is extremely unusual. We make a mistake when we fail to appreciate the strength of the psychological needs.

How long we can endure need frustration will vary from person to person depending on the strength of the need and our capacity to satisfy it. But if the frustration starts running into days, we *feel* the pain of this frustration acutely just as we *feel* the pleasure that is always present when we are in effective control of our lives. *Feel* is the correct word here because, assuming we do not use addicting drugs, *how we feel is the most accurate information we can get as to whether or not we are in control of our lives.* What is important here is to understand that we cannot escape from the pain of being unable to satisfy our genetic assignments. Our needs are as fixed biologically as the movement of the stars is fixed in space.

Not knowing or not accepting control theory, boss-managers act as if the people they manage can somehow suspend their needs or subordinate them to the needs of the boss when they are at work. At their best, bosses are pleased if the people they manage enjoy themselves at work, but most do not manage as if this is important to them. At their worst, they manage in a way that workers find almost impossible to satisfy their needs to the extent they would like. Since most bossed workers believe they need their job to survive, they are willing to put up with frustration, but they don't like it and they will rarely do more than they have to do to keep the job. Lead-managers know that doing quality work never crosses the mind of a frustrated worker.

Frustrated workers blame the boss and they become and remain adversaries. It is not possible to be in contact with an adversary and not act on that frustration. At work, this is the most destructive of all situations. Overtly or covertly, depending on how much power the worker perceives the boss to have, the worker fights the boss. To fight someone when there is little hope of winning wastes a lot of energy. People say that working on a frustrating job is draining and this is a precise description of exactly what is happening—bossing drains energy from what is available to do the job.

Bosses worry that if they give power to the workers they, themselves, will lose power. The exact opposite is true. Workers are so appreciative of getting some power (to them some control) that they respect the person who gives it to them. This will be covered more in Chapter 7 when I explain the quality world that exists in all our heads.

Let us look again at the four points that describe a boss manager. Essentially they are:

1. The boss sets the task and the standards for what the workers are to do, usually without consulting the workers. Bosses do not compromise; the worker has to adjust to the job as the boss defines it or suffer any consequences the boss determines.

2. The boss usually tells, rather than shows, the workers how the work is to be done and rarely asks for their input as to how it might possibly be done better.

3. The boss, or someone the boss designates, inspects the work. Because the boss does not involve the workers in this evaluation, they do only enough to get by; they rarely even think of doing what is required for quality.

4. When workers resist, as they almost always do in a variety of ways, all of which compromise quality, the boss uses coercion (usually punishment) almost exclusively to try to make them do as they are told. In so doing, the boss creates a workplace in which the workers and the managers are adversaries. Bosses think that this adversarial situation is the way it should be.

As you see, none of these points is concerned with giving any friendship, fun, freedom, and especially power to the worker. Together these points send a clear message from the boss: if you don't do what I say, I will punish you in whatever way I can. And many bosses figure out subtle ways to punish workers that are especially painful. The reader may say that I am overstating the case, that bosses are rarely this bad. This may be true, but to succeed in persuading the workers to do the quality work that is needed today, they must be seen as leaders—benevolent dictators are not enough.

Look at the four elements of lead-managing and see how much more the leader is concerned with the workers' needs, especially their need for power:

1. Lead-managers engage the workers in an ongoing honest discussion of both the cost and the quality of the work that is needed for the company to be successful. They not only listen but they also encourage their workers to give them any input that will improve quality and lower costs.

2. The lead-manager (or someone designated by her) shows or models the job, so that the worker who is to do the job can see exactly what the manager expects. The lead-manager works to increase the workers' sense of control over the work they do.

3. The lead-manager eliminates most inspectors and inspection. He teaches the workers to inspect or to evaluate their own work for quality with the understanding that they know a great deal, almost always more than anyone else, about both what high-quality work is and how to produce it economically.

4. The lead-manager continually teaches the workers that the essence of quality is constant improvement.

To help them, he makes it clear that he believes his main job is to be a facilitator. This means he is doing all he can to provide them with the best tools and workplace as well as a friendly, noncoercive, nonadversarial atmosphere in which to do the job.

This is obviously a different style of managing in which leaders make a constant effort to combine the requirements of the job with the needs of the workers. The quality of work produced by leadership[5] is so far superior to what is produced by bossing that it is difficult even to compare the former with the latter.

Keeping the needs in mind, we must now go on and explain the next element of control theory: how we behave. To lead successfully, a leader must be aware of the fact that behavior is much more complicated than most of us realize.

CHAPTER SIX

All Behavior Is Total Behavior

As explained in Chapter 5, the cause of all behavior is our constant attempt to choose what we believe will *best* satisfy our needs. Therefore, if a worker does quality work, he chooses to do it because it is more satisfying than if he did not make this choice. Assuming he knows how to do quality work but he does not do it, this too is a choice. This is because what he is asked to do and/or how he is asked to do it is not satisfying enough of his needs to persuade him to make the effort.

A lead-manager will not use this knowledge of control theory to accuse a worker of choosing to do less than he is capable of doing, because doing this will only make the problem worse. The accused worker will get defensive and deny the accusation vehemently. He will never admit that he chose to do something shoddy or thoughtless.

Workers will say, "I didn't realize I was doing this," or "I don't know how it happened that I did that," or "I couldn't help it," or "What else could I have done?," as if a better behavior were impossible. The manager's main task is to persuade workers to expend the effort to choose to do the quality work that they are almost all capable of doing. To accomplish this task, the lead-manager knows this choice is always possible. It will, however, take skillful managing to persuade some workers to make these quality choices. The best way for managers to gain these skills is to learn how control theory explains behavior, an explanation that is more complicated than most people realize.

To begin to understand behavior, the best place to start is to look it up in the dictionary where it will be defined very simply as (1) activity and (2) a response to a stimulus. The first definition is incomplete; the second, as explained in Chapter 5, is wrong. While every behavior includes some activity, control theory is unique in explaining that behavior encompasses *much more* than activity. *It is a combination of four separate components of which activity (or acting) is only one.* The other three are *thinking, feeling,* and *physiology.*

For example, when we choose to run, the physical activity of moving our legs is one component; what we think about as we run is another; how we feel as we run is the third; and what our heart, lungs, and muscles are doing are major parts of the fourth, of our physiology. Therefore, control theory explains that all behavior is more accurately called *total behavior—total* because it is always *the sum of four separate components*: actions, thoughts, feelings, and physiology. While I will discuss these components separately, *they are actually never separate.* Each component is always present as a part of the whole or total behavior.

As long as we are conscious, two of the four components, acting and thinking, are almost totally voluntary; the other two, feeling and physiology, are rarely under our voluntary control. For example, we regularly choose the total behavior of eating. First our automatic physiology causes us to experience hunger pangs. We then think about eating, and soon sit down and eat. We choose this total behavior knowing we will feel better and be healthier. If we decide to lose weight, painful as a weight-loss diet may be, it is often a choice based on our desire to be healthier or more attractive. We do not choose the pain, but we know from experience we cannot avoid it.

As important as our feelings are, often we pay little attention to them. As long as we don't feel strongly, we tend to be more aware of our actions and thoughts. For example, if you are deep in thought while playing chess you might even skip lunch. You are so engrossed that you are not even aware of being hungry. But when we feel very good or very bad, we pay a great deal of attention to how we feel; in fact, we are often much more aware of our feelings than of the other three components.

It is safe to say that of the four components *how we feel is the most important.* This is because our feelings tell us if the behavior we are choosing is effective or ineffective. If it is highly satisfying to one or more needs, we feel very good and believe we have chosen an effective behavior. If it is frustrating, we will feel bad and immediately realize that what we have chosen is not effective. For example, we choose total behavior "A" over "B" or "C" because we believe that, in the predictable future, "A" will feel good or, at least, better than any other behavior that comes to mind. Therefore, in choosing what we do, we are always trying to continue or increase what feels good and to discontinue or reduce what feels bad.

From the manager's standpoint, if an employee feels bad, the manager's main responsibility is to help him to better satisfy his needs, which usually means to act and think more effectively on the job. For example, you could team him with a skilled, friendly worker, suggest he improve his skills by taking training the company offers, ask him to take charge of a small project so that he experiences a little more recognition or, if it seems that this is needed, encourage him to tell you what may be on his mind.

But, regardless of what it is the employee needs to do to feel better, when he succeeds, what he has done is change from one total behavior to a better one. To do that will always require that he change how he acts and thinks, so it is on actions and thoughts that a lead-manager focuses. He accepts feelings and physiology and understands how important they are, but he concentrates on what can be changed. Therefore, the geometric axiom that applies perfectly to the concept of total behavior is *the whole is the sum of the parts,* and its corollary is *if you change any part, you change the whole.*

To make this clear, suppose you choose to take a walk, a choice based on your belief that doing this will feel better than anything else you can do at this time. You first think, "I'll walk," and then you engage in the activity of walking. As you walk, you may think a variety of thoughts, but you pretty much choose whatever you think. You may let your mind wander and may succeed in avoiding any particular thoughts, but it is your choice to let it wander. You can, however, stop its wandering any time you wish by choosing to think of something specific.

Ordinarily, you don't choose how you feel. For example, when you walk, your physiology is automatically adjusted to the demands of the activity, and how you feel—good, bad, or indifferent—will depend on how satisfying the walk turns out to be. If it starts to rain and you get wet, you may be miserable. You didn't choose the rain, but neither did you seem to be able to choose not to feel miserable when you come home wet and bedraggled. On the other hand, if, as soon as it starts to rain, a good friend comes along in a car and you have a pleasant visit while he drives you home, you will say that the walk turned out well. You did not choose to have your friend come along, but when he did, it was impossible not to choose to feel good.

It is also very important to understand that, *on occasion, it is possible to choose to feel bad, although most of the time we are unaware that we are actually making this choice.* The painful choice is based on our belief that, if we did not make it, we could feel even worse or we might choose to do something that increases the problem. For example, as miserable as it is, most of us are capable of choosing to feel depressed when we mess up an important assignment at work. We are not aware of this choice, but it is still based on the idea that our manager will treat us better if we are suffering. He may even excuse our poor work or offer to get us some help. If we didn't choose the depression, there is the possibility that we might choose to get angry and unfairly attack others, which would make the whole situation much worse.

Very early in life we learn to make these miserable choices when we mess up. For example, we learn to cry and be distraught when we spill our milk and *we are quite aware that this is a choice.* We may actually think it's funny, but we know that if we laughed, our mother would "kill" us. *As we grow, we become less and less aware that these are choices, because if we continued to be aware that we are even capable of choosing pain and misery, we would feel stupid and ashamed, both highly frustrating to our need for power.* By the time we are adults, we may be totally unaware that these are choices. But if a manager is aware of what is going on, he can help many employees make better, more need-satisfying choices.

Among the common forms of misery we learn to choose, although we are almost always unaware that

they are choices, are depression, anxiety, common illnesses such as colds and stomach upsets, some allergic
conditions such as hives, and some physically based
pains such as headaches and backaches. But these
choices are complicated in that once we choose one or
more of these miseries *there is nothing we can do
directly to stop the pain or the illness because we are
not aware that we are making a choice.* A doctor may
give us a drug such as Valium that, in altering our physiology, may make us feel better for a while. But drugs
are rarely a solution to the problem *because they do not
deal with the basic need frustration that was the cause
of the miserable choice in the first place.* And drugs are
often addicting, which may soon vastly increase our
problem.

Aware or not, people who make these painful
choices fail to understand that they are actually choosing a *total behavior* that is made up of more than the
feeling or the unhealthy physiology. It also includes acting and thinking, *and it is these components that we can
always choose to change.* If you are managing a worker
who is depressed and doing a poor job, and you suspect
that he is choosing to be depressed to avoid being held
responsible for the poor quality of his work, you will
know that he cannot help himself. He is no more aware
that he has a choice to act and think more effectively
than he is aware that he is choosing the misery.

Your job is to talk with him supportively, especially
to listen to him, and persuade him that he can actually
do something better on the job if he will choose to make

the effort. In the beginning, you look for an area in which he has competence and, with your support, can experience success. Tell him you will check on his progress to see if he needs more help, but you do not want to hear why he can't do it; you believe he can. If he does, he will gain confidence, continue to improve, and with these new and more effective acting and thinking choices, he will stop choosing the pain and misery of depression. Later, you might give him this book, so that he can learn what he did that worked.

What this illustrates is that we can always choose more need-satisfying actions and thoughts and, when we do, we will give up the old self-destructive choices that failed to satisfy our needs. From the standpoint of management, these choices cost companies huge sums of money and always reduce quality. As much as the loss of the money is bad, the reduction in quality in a competitive market is far worse. Lead-managers who learn control theory and become more and more aware that we are capable of choosing to feel bad will not misuse this knowledge to be punitive. Lead-managers are never punitive.

It is also important to know that it is rare to employ many people without having a few who abuse alcohol. They are risking their job in a desperate effort to feel better. Using "alcoholic thinking," they often go so far as to bring a bottle to work and sneak drinks on the job. To implement this decision, they must think and act but, due to the alcohol, they are totally unaware that their ability to act and think effectively is now seriously impaired.

If you were a boss-manager and you caught an employee drinking on the job, you might threaten to fire him unless he stopped. You would have told him to stop doing what he was choosing to do, but you would not have helped him make a better choice. Still frustrated, he would likely get angry and rationalize that you, not his choice to drink, are the problem. Confronted with threats from a boss-manager and unable to figure out how to change, he may drink even more heavily, file a stress complaint, or report sick and spend a lot of company money on medical care that will not address the real problem.

Lead-managers may also tell an employee who is alcoholic that his job is at risk, but they will then go on and help him make a better choice. As long as an alcoholic keeps drinking, it is unlikely that he will choose a better total behavior and he may think he is doomed to be a drunk. Lead-managers who have learned control theory *know that we cannot just stop doing anything. All we can do is change to a more effective behavior.* To do this, we often need help.

As the manager of this employee, you must be willing to counsel him at least to the extent of persuading him to seek professional help. Suppose he chooses to attend AA regularly, and as he works the AA program, he chooses to stop drinking and once again is an effective employee. What he has done is much more than just stop drinking. He has changed his total behavior and is now thinking and acting much more effectively, because he is no longer suffering from the physiologic impairment brought on by his choosing to drink. Healthy now, he tells you he hasn't felt this good in years. As this is a very pressing problem in many companies, I will explain more about how to deal with alcoholic employees in Part Three of this book.

CHAPTER SEVEN

The Quality World

Since we must satisfy our needs in the real world, we have to be equipped with a way to find out what that world really is. This leads to what at first glance seems to be a silly question: How do we know that there even is such a thing as the real world? William James, the father of American psychology, recognized that this was an important question and, to get his students thinking about it in the 1890s, he would query them as follows: "If a baby were born with no senses (meaning no vision, hearing, touch, taste, or smell) and was kept alive, as should be possible, what would be inside his mind when he reached eighteen years of age?"

What James was driving at was the fact that the only way we can find out there is such a thing as the real world is that we are born with the capacity to sense it. Having no senses, whatever was in that eighteen-year-old's head would be restricted to what he was able to imagine; he would have no inkling of what actually existed. Helen Keller proved we don't have to have all of our senses to find out that there is a real world all around us and we, ourselves, are part of it, but we have to have some of them: she had touch, taste, and smell. For this book, however, I am going to assume the readers have them all.

It is important to know that our senses, by themselves, do not tell us the world exists. They are just the outposts of a complicated perceptual system that exists in our brain, and it is through the workings of this whole system that we actually discover the world. How this is done is too complicated for this nontechnical book, but there is no doubt we do it easily. By the time we are a few years old, we are already capable of recognizing most of what goes on around us enough so that we can name things. Very early in life, we become especially capable of recognizing and naming people that feel very good such as mother and things that feel good such as ice cream. So very early, we become especially interested in anything we deal with that feels very good.

It is from this interest that we build a special place in our memory that I call our *quality world*. In it we store what we have discovered that feels very good, much of it as pictures of people, places, and things and as word pictures of need-satisfying ideas or beliefs. We do not know—if we don't learn control theory we may never know—that this knowledge is related to highly need-satisfying experiences. What we do know, and we will never forget, is that these are the people, places, things, and ideas that we want to make contact with as we live our lives because, when we do, it feels so good.

This specific knowledge that makes up our quality world becomes the core of our lives. We try to add to it as we live, but we don't add anything that doesn't feel very good. We also remove things from this world when they no longer feel good, and once we do, we lose interest in them, sometimes even to the point of disliking them strongly as often happens when we get divorced.

To use control theory language, what all of us functioning as control systems are always trying to do is control the real world so that it is as close as we can make it to our quality world. Thus, as much as we are trying to satisfy our needs, it is not our needs themselves that actually drive our behavior. Rather it is the specific, highly need-satisfying knowledge that we store in our relatively small quality world that is the driving force of our lives. For example, a child does not want "love"; she wants a "loving mother." It is through the loving mother that she gets the love she wants. We almost never search for abstractions such as love and power. Our quest is always for very specific, concrete entities, such as mother when we try to satisfy our need for love.

The quality world allows us to define the concept of quality: *quality is whatever we choose to store in our quality world.* For each of us that and nothing else is quality, which means that each of us has total control over what we put into our quality world. We, and we only, make that important decision. Because it is impossible that all of us would ever agree on anything that is so universal that we would all put it into our quality worlds, there can never be an absolute definition of quality. But since we are of the same species and many of us live in similar cultures, much of what is in our quality worlds is similar or the same. If I manufacture a successful product such as Coca Cola, what makes it successful is that I have succeeded in making something that a great many people have decided to put into their quality worlds.

When I say that our quality world is the most important part of our lives, I mean, for example, that we do not listen attentively to people who are not in this world and we do not want a product that is not in it or that we are not considering putting into it. We will not believe an idea or accept a value that is not in our quality world. If it is in this world, it is quality to us even if it is destructive, for example, alcohol is very much a part of the quality worlds of all alcoholics.

If I am to manage successfully, it is necessary that I convince the people I manage to put what I ask them to do into their quality worlds. But to do this, it is almost a given that the people I manage have to first put me into their quality worlds. Deming does not teach this concept, but how he recommends we manage, what I call lead-management, is the most effective way to manage people so that they put both the manager and/or the product or service into their quality worlds. Lead-managers succeed in gaining access to the quality worlds of the people they manage, because they are sensitive to the workers' needs.

Bosses who coerce, threaten, and do not seem to care about the needs of the workers are the last people workers will put into their quality worlds. This is the short, accurate, control theory explanation of why bosses have so much trouble getting workers to do quality work.

It is possible that a worker will do quality work because he finds the work, itself, satisfying regardless of how he is treated. But as work gets broken down into more and more pieces and fewer and fewer workers have access to the finished product, it is more how the worker is managed than the work itself that determines whether the worker will do the quality work necessary for a company to be competitive. *A company should base all decisions on how well each decision has a chance both to persuade and then to maintain (1) the company, (2) the managers, (3) the products and services, and (4) the customers in the workers' quality worlds.* If most of the workers put all four into their quality worlds and the company keeps improving the product while keeping its cost competitive, that company will prosper.

Our automobile industry is a classic example of an industry whose managers have not persuaded enough workers at all levels to put the company, the managers, the product, and the customers into their quality worlds. This has led to the severe decline in the quality of many American cars and it is this decline that has led many previously good customers to remove these cars from their quality worlds. *Keeping its products and services in the quality worlds of its customers is the true bottom line of every company.* Once customers decide to take a company product or service out of their quality worlds, there is very little that most companies can do to persuade them to change their minds. Our auto companies have lost their places in too many of their former customers' quality worlds to foreign competition. It is proving very difficult and expensive to get back what they once had so completely.

We don't usually take something out of our quality worlds unless we are convinced that there is something else to replace it. Many customers are loyal to an American product because "Made in the USA" is a strong part of their quality worlds. The decision to put something into our quality worlds is based on a multitude of factors: the strongest factor is the quality of the product itself. If we depend on advertisers to sell the product through celebrities, an appeal to patriotism, a low price, or a picture of a bunch of young, happy people using the product, they may succeed for a while. But a long-term satisfied customer is by far the best advertising there is.

It is the same for managers. They must show a real concern for the workers' needs. Slogans, prizes, or sales contests will not keep a poor product or service profitable. To do this, managers have to learn to do something that many managers have not considered doing: put the workers they manage into their quality worlds. If they refuse to do this, it is unlikely they will be able to become lead-managers. What I am talking about here is a two-way street: both workers and managers must put each other into their quality worlds. Managers who are unwilling to walk both up and down this street will not be capable of managing for quality.

The needs, total behavior, and quality world are the heart of control theory. If you understand this much, you are well on your way to knowing what is needed to become a lead-manager. There are still a few concepts to be explained that I will cover in Chapter 8, but if you understand this much, you will have no trouble learning what remains.

CHAPTER EIGHT

What Actually Starts Our Behavior and the Cause of Our Creativity

In the previous chapter, I explained that the knowledge that is stored in our quality worlds is the "picture" of what we are trying to accomplish with our behavior. For example, previously I said that we do not answer a phone because it rings. All the ring provides us with is the information that there is someone on the other end who wants to talk to someone on our end. We answer only if there is a picture of answering a phone and talking to whomever is on the other end as a need-satisfying activity in our quality world. If we did not have that picture, we would never answer a ringing phone.

The actual reason we answer is when the phone rings there is a large *difference* between what we want, to talk to someone on the other end, and what we have, just the phone ringing. *It is this difference between what we want, which is stored in our quality world, and what is now happening in the real world that is the specific cause of all our behavior.*

For a worker to do quality work, a manager who is in the worker's quality world must ask him to look carefully at what he is doing and evaluate it in terms of what he believes is quality. If this evaluation tells the worker that the work he is doing is not quality, the manager must then ask him to compare it with what he knows is quality, which is in his quality world. When he makes that comparison, he will immediately see that there is a specific difference between the quality he wants and what he is now producing. He will then be motivated to work harder and soon move from "good enough" work to quality work. He should also be asked to keep evaluating what he is doing and to keep improving as he will also be asked to put the idea of constant improvement into his quality world.

This is why Deming stresses constant improvement, because he knows that quality cannot be static. Once a worker puts the pictures of quality work and constant improvement into his quality world, he will have no choice but to work hard, especially if he has a picture of the manager and customer in that world. As he does, he will work to produce a better and better product or service. The result is constant improvement, but to assure that this will happen it is necessary that managers give their workers some important, additional support.

If they are to put a picture of continually improving quality work into their quality worlds, workers need managers to give them a tangible gesture of appreciation for doing this. Specifically, they want managers to *trust* them to evaluate their own work. The workers know they have this trust when the managers accept that they are producing quality. What I am describing is the evolution from bossing to leading, from checking all the workers do to trusting them to do the very best they can. *Once this trust is established, quality in that organization is also established.* From this point, the only concern of workers and managers is to agree on a fair way to compensate the workers for their contribution.

Constant improvement requires more than hard work on the part of the worker. It also requires that the worker be creative and add this creativity to his output. To assure that he will do this, the lead-manager must be willing to listen to him if he wants to do something new. Boss-managers do not often think about creativity, especially as it may arise from a worker. In the minds of boss-managers, workers are supposed to do what they are told with no exceptions. Boss-managers tend to think concretely about the work and, to them, creativity is something mysterious that is only available to a few special people.

This is not true. Control theory teaches that we are all creative and that this creativity becomes most available to us when we feel as if we are in control or when there is only a small difference between the way we want to be treated and the way we are treated. Under these relaxed circumstances, we all tend to be creative, but the catch is that there is no guarantee that our creativity will be usable on the job. All that is guaranteed is that, when lead-management is succeeding and there is only a small difference between the quality we are accomplishing and the quality we want, we tend to become increasingly aware of both our creativity and how we might use it to improve what we do.

If we become aware of a very creative idea or procedure, we will not try to put it into practice unless we are also confident that we will not be put down for what we are suggesting. Therefore, a lead-manager is highly supportive in that he makes a point of telling his workers that they should feel free to tell him about any good ideas they may have. He will listen. But a good lead-manager goes even further. He observes his satisfied workers and looks for creativity. When he sees it, even in an embryonic form, he talks with the worker and asks her to explain what she is doing and encourages her to go further with it.

Therefore, a lead-manager who understands control theory will also understand creativity. He will know that it is always available and no one can predict where or when valuable, usable new ideas will make an appearance. Everything he does will encourage workers to pay attention to their creativity and share it with him and others who might be interested. He will tell the workers they should not be hasty in judging the value of a new idea: "Think about it and do not hesitate to share it with me even if on the surface it seems to have little value. It could have a spark that together we could kindle to the benefit of all."

This impresses workers. They spread the word that the manager is interested in new ideas and turn loose the kind of creativity that leads to gains in quality that are not possible without this tangible support. If we are not capable, as boss-managers usually are not, of tapping the creativity of those we manage, we will not come close to discovering the new and better ways to do a job or solve a problem that are the core of quality.

Bosses put a damper on creativity. They know how the job should be done and there is only one way: their way. Their workers tend to work for a paycheck and their pay is the main difference between what they want and what they have. Bossed workers tend to pay no attention to their creativity because they know it is not wanted; no one will listen to them anyway. Stifling creativity, which is easily stifled—a derisive look may do it forever—may be the worst effect of bosses. They make it impossible to reach the level of quality that is only available to lead-managers who are aware that how they treat workers will either tap or turn off their creativity.

But even worse happens when workers are bossed and stifled. Since how they want to be treated is so different from how they are treated, they use their creativity to bolster their efforts in the war between workers and bosses that is the product of the adversarial relationship that always exists between these two traditional enemies. Not only is effort lost in this battle but, when workers are very fearful for their job, this creativity can appear as sickness or as physical pains and aches in the fearful, frustrated workers. Many vague or flu-like illnesses as well as pains and aches like headaches and backaches are created by frustrated workers getting physiologically creative on the job.

It is well known that a company that is led by managers whose workers have them in their quality worlds have much lower medical expenses, absenteeism, accidents, and work disruptions than workers who are bossed. Bossing leads to dissatisfaction, which causes expensive waste and misery. The failure of many of our major industries to produce competitive products is the price that we pay for bossing workers. If managers would be willing to learn control theory, it is a price we would not have to pay.

PART THREE

Putting It All Together

Introduction

If you have read this far, I know from experience that many of you are saying to yourselves, "Lead-management is too soft; it bends too far in the direction of the workers. I will lose so much authority that the workers won't respect me and I won't have the power to act decisively when problems arise." If your company has the market locked up, you can afford to think this way and this book is not for you. If, however, you are not in this situation, and few of you are, then your difficulty with lead-management is not that it is too soft. *It is that you find it difficult to conceptualize how much you have to do to achieve quality.*

Nowhere is this difficulty to conceptualize quality better illustrated than in Chapter 2 of Dave Barry's 1992 book, *Dave Barry Does Japan.*[1] He explains that he travels frequently with his wife and small son and, for the past ten years when he has reserved a hotel room in the United States, he has asked when making the reservation that the hotel put a roll-away bed for his son in the room. Almost always, the day before arrival, his wife calls the hotel to remind them that the roll-away has been ordered.

He then says, "There has never, not once in ten years, in dozens and dozens of hotels, been an actual folding bed in our room when we got there." Not only has it not been there but to get one at night when they usually arrive is difficult. The help is surly and feels put upon to do something that is not their job. They make it obvious that the bed should have been ordered earlier while still expecting a tip. He goes on to say, "In Japan, the bed was always there, in every hotel, when we checked in. This may seem minor to you but, to us, it was a miracle."

This story illustrates my point. In good hotels in our country—Dave Barry stays in good hotels—the managers cannot even conceptualize the level of service, which to Dave Barry, when he got it, "was a miracle." I realize that miracles are hard to conceptualize, but this is exactly what every business in the United States that has a competitor must learn to do. It is not to "good enough" or to "a little better" but to this level of quality that this book is addressed. If we, as managers, cannot persuade the people we manage, as our hotel managers obviously believe they cannot, to put service into their quality worlds, our ability to compete will continue to decline.

We have overwhelming evidence in this recession that the losses and layoffs in prestigious companies such as Sears and IBM are caused by the lack of creative improvement that will always occur when the top stops listening to those struggling at the cutting edge where buying, selling, and servicing take place. Competitors who practice continuous, creative improvement will race ahead. Customers are taking these troubled companies out of their quality worlds and, as business declines, these companies are laying off workers to compete for price. *But ruthless cost cutting alienates the very workers who must be depended on to do the quality work, which is the only thing that can restore the competitiveness that has been lost*—a catch 22 from which some formerly great companies may not recover.

Many of these companies have been run by semi-benevolent dictators who managed well enough in lightly competitive markets but could not compete when the competition got tough. Today, we are mostly hiring in industries such as fast food where price rather than quality are the norm, but even here, as competition heats up, only the higher-quality companies will survive. These jobs, however, don't pay enough to support the economy; we won't fry our way out of this recession.

CHAPTER NINE

Criticism

So far I have mostly explained what a lead-manager should do. Now I want to focus on what a lead-manager should not do: *criticize*. No matter how badly an employee performs, it is unwise to criticize his or her performance. Difficult as it may be for you to accept, I do not believe that there is such a thing as constructive criticism.

This does not mean that the manager accepts poor performance or fails to deal with it. On the contrary, a lead-manager does not let anything slide that she believes could be improved. She deals with it as soon as she can, but she does so without using anything the employee can reasonably construe as criticism. In fact, it would be good practice for all lead-managers to post a sign in their workplace, with their signature prominently displayed at the bottom, stating clearly something like the following:

In this department, I attempt to help all employees solve all problems that either I or they become aware of, but in doing so, I will not criticize, put down, or punish. I encourage all employees to do the same with me and with each other.

Criticism occurs in many forms, all of which are destructive to quality. Not only can it be verbal but it can also be a gesture; tone of voice; look of disgust or disdain; refusal to talk with, listen, or see someone; or an obviously insincere attempt to deal with a problem. Criticism should be defined as anything an employee interprets as criticism, because that employee will act as if it were and quality will always suffer.

We accept that it is very difficult for a manager who sees a multitude of shortcomings as he walks around to do as suggested here. It seems so right to call the employee in and explain how much better he could do his job if he would do it the manager's way. This certainly does not seem to be critical, but even this will be interpreted by almost all employees as criticism. Even if they are aware that they are doing something wrong, they still resent being told about it, even politely. And they will channel that resentment into resistance, which means that energy that could be used to improve what they are doing will be dissipated in this resistance and, again, quality will suffer. It is criticism from the manager that is the largest cause of the energy-wasting, adversarial relationships that exist between too many employees and boss-managers.

Control theory explains clearly that none of us will

put anyone who criticizes us, or what we do, into our quality worlds. We won't because when we are criticized, accurately or not, we feel we have lost power, friendship, and the freedom to act as we think best. It is as simple as that. It does not matter that the criticism was warranted or that, in private, the employee agrees he was doing something wrong.

This is never a question of right or wrong; it is a question of how the employee perceives the manager's actions, and from the employee's standpoint he will perceive any criticism as a *barrier* to admitting both the manager and what the manager wants him to do into his quality world. To a lead-manager, the most important thing he must do if he wants quality work is to treat the employees in such a way that he is admitted into their quality worlds. To achieve this, he focuses on eliminating criticism from all he does with everyone in the company: subordinates, equals, and superiors. It may be easier for you to understand what I am talking about if you think about how you would approach a superior whom you believed was doing something wrong. It isn't likely that you would directly criticize him.

Lead-managers should approach all employees who need to improve what they are doing the same way. They should say something such as, "It seems to me that there may be a problem here and I would like to talk with you and see if we agree." The emphasis is on *we,* not you or me. Further he states, "If we agree there is a problem, I want to look at what each of us can do to solve it." If the employee does not see it as a problem, the lead-manager should be ready to admit that there may not be a problem by saying, "Let's talk further. You may be right. I will be happy to agree if you can explain that no problem exists."

If the employee is willing to admit that there may be a problem, as most will, the lead-manager should say, "Let's see what each of us is doing that may be causing the problem." He does not say that it is all or even part the employee's fault. In fact, as he talks to the employee, he will never even intimate it is anyone's fault. He will ignore the idea of fault altogether and emphasize from start to finish that all he is interested in is solving the problem. He is not even interested in the history of the problem unless that history is vital for its solution.

The manager is also willing to involve anyone else, even a whole team, in the solution to the problem. Often the employee will admit that there is a problem, but to avoid criticism she will not admit that she is at fault. It is usually someone else; the manager is talking to the wrong person. The lead-manager will listen and then say, "Okay, let's get that person involved and will you help me explain what's wrong and what needs to be done to correct it." He reemphasizes that he is not looking to criticize or find fault; all he is looking for is a way to solve the problem.

At the same time, the lead-manager will caution an employee who has a lot to do with the problem but who wants to implicate more people that they may end up with a bigger problem than they have now. The purpose of this approach is to involve only the person who is most associated with the problem in solving it. To do this and avoid being seen as critical, I suggest you say something like, "I think we can solve this. You know what the problem is and you have a lot of skills. Let's see if we can put it to rest without involving a lot of other people." This allows the employee to work on the problem in a way that he escapes blame and criticism. In doing so, he can put all his energy into solving it.

The lead-manager is trying to set up a *no-fault, no-criticism policy.* Once this policy is set, the lead-managed employees will tend to do much more evaluating than bossed employees. It is not that bossed employees don't evaluate now; they do. But what they evaluate is everything and everyone but themselves. It is always someone else's fault, because in a boss-managed environment their main concern is to avoid blame or criticism.

In the nonblaming, noncriticizing lead-management environment, they will feel free to evaluate their work, quality will increase, and they will solve problems by themselves without even going to the manager. In this trusting atmosphere, they will work together and, in doing so, will get away from the situation caused by criticizing and punishing in which each employee protects her own turf even if it is to the detriment of the company.

I realize this is not easy to do. We live in a stimulus-response, blaming, criticizing, fault-finding, punishing society in which people find it very hard to trust each

other. Quality is built on cooperation and *for coopera-*
tion to exist there must be trust. We may not be capable
of changing a whole society—Deming has not accomplished this in Japan where the present worldwide
recession is throwing some light on the conspicuous
consumption that is endemic to the grandiose thinking,
corruption, and lack of planning for prosperity that is
suddenly so apparent in that country. *What we can*
learn from the Japanese is how to manage workers so
that they do quality work. In other areas, we could both
teach each other a great deal about how to live sensibly.

CHAPTER TEN

Supervising Noncoercively

While managing workers is commonly considered to be the process of telling them what to do, a lead-manager always softens this approach to the noncoercive technique of asking. To most employees there is an implication of coercion in "telling" that is absent in "asking." As I help people learn the skills of lead-managing, I find that, next to teaching self-evaluation, learning to supervise noncoercively, for example, asking rather than telling, is the hardest part of the process. Fueled by a lifetime of exposure, starting in our homes, accelerating in our schools, and peaking in many of our work experiences, coercion has become so ingrained that it is literally a part of what most of us consider to be common sense. Even though it is so destructive to the goal of quality, it seems so right.

For years I have been teaching my method of noncoercive counseling, reality therapy, to thousands of people. Most of these people are counselors or teachers and do not think of themselves as managers. It is obvious, however, that most of what teachers do is *manage* because, similar to business, they also have an agenda for their students and are trying to get them to accept this agenda. In the case of counselors, many of whom counsel delinquents or alcoholics, I have no difficulty teaching that coercion does not work. They accept the idea that they must persuade the people they counsel to put them into their quality worlds or their counseling will be ineffective.

When we work with teachers, it is apparent that students are much more difficult to manage successfully than people who work for a living. Most teachers are strict boss-managers whose philosophy is centered on coercion: behave and learn as I tell you or face low grades or failure. Students in school learn a variety of ways to resist this bossing, so when they leave school and go to work, they are well prepared to resist the threats and punishment that continue as a natural part of the work process.

Therefore, what we help both counselors and teachers learn is much more than counseling and teaching; it is how to manage successfully and it is fully applicable to business. In fact, less skills are required of business managers than of counselors and teachers because, unlike students, employees get paid and mostly see what they are asked to do as useful. Because of this, they tend to want to do a good job much more than a student wants to learn history or an alcoholic wants to stop drinking. So while both school and business require lead-management, business is by far the easier place to put it into practice.

CREATING THE LEAD-MANAGERIAL ENVIRONMENT

Specifically, to deal with people noncoercively means to make work a talking and listening place, especially listening. More than anything else, this helps the workers feel as if they have some power, and the more workers feel empowered the more likely they are to do quality work. That workers who feel powerless will not do quality work is as axiomatic as a straight line is the shortest distance between two points.

When managers talk with workers, they should solicit their opinions on almost anything. Once the workers get the idea that the manager is interested in what they have to say, it will be natural for them to talk about the job and give their opinion on all aspects of what they are doing. As managers listen and talk with the workers, they should begin, as soon as possible, to bring up the subject of quality. It is important that the manager try to establish an environment where quality is both frequently and freely discussed and related to the job to be done.

Managers should also explain that they are now attempting to lead instead of boss. For a long time workers who have been bossed all their lives will tend to see even a relaxed, friendly, conversational manager as a boss. It takes time for them to realize that what is now being done is really much different from bossing. When a manager asks the workers over and over what he can do to help them to do a better job, and the manager does much of what the workers ask, they will see that he practices what he preaches. As they do, they will become aware that this manager is much different from the usual boss.

Managers should also make clear that they do not criticize or punish. They accomplish this by not doing these things and by talking with workers directly on this subject. Tell them straight out that what we do is solve problems: we believe that criticism or punishment increases problems; it never solves them. Lead-managers tell workers they do not see them as adversaries, as people who have to be pushed to accomplish what the manager wants. They drive this point home by not punishing workers in situations where, by tradition, workers are almost always punished.

For example, a worker misses a day's work and expects to be docked a day's pay or have to lie and use a day of sick leave. The lead-manager knows the worker was not sick; it may have been the first day of hunting season and he is aware the worker is an avid hunter. Instead of being critical or punitive, the manager asks the worker if he can work out a way to make up the work or plan with the manager in the future so the worker can be excused on a few special days. The manager continually emphasizes that his goal is quality work; he is not interested in chaining workers to the job if there is a more flexible way to get it done. He shows through this approach that the worker's welfare is important to him and that he is not rigid as long as quality and productivity are not compromised and union rules do not prevent this flexibility.

In nonunion workplaces, lead-managers do not wait

for the workers to ask for a raise. As quality and productivity rise, the manager should approach all the workers individually and in small groups to explain the company wants to work out a way to share the profits that have been earned through their quality work. As Deming teaches, a statistical record of productivity and quality is kept so everyone knows what has been gained. Groups, rather than individuals, should be rewarded; individual rewards should be limited to one-time bonuses for good suggestions. What this fair share may be is a subject for negotiation, but a lead-manager would work out an agreement with the workers on how their pay can be tied to productivity and profits. Bosses do not do this. They use raises to coerce in ways that are often capricious and beyond the workers' control.

Finally, the lead-manager never fails to emphasize that the work must be constantly improved. He is relentless in his conviction that his employees are as good or better than any workers anywhere. The lead-manager should personify the idea that we will never give up no matter what problem arises. Together we can find solutions to almost anything. The work environment is totally "*we* can do it." Coercion does not exist.

CHAPTER ELEVEN

Solving Problems with Counseling

The thrust of this whole book so far is to explain how lead-managers create workplaces where serious problems are unlikely to arise. But no matter how good a job they do, both work and personal problems will occur regularly. This is an organizational fact of life. To assure quality, these problems must be addressed. If the problems are work related, they should be handled as soon as the lead-manager becomes aware of them. Delay only makes things worse. If they are not directly work related, such as difficulties at home, drinking, drug abuse, or financial distress, it may be difficult to tell if the employee's work is being affected. Since there is a good chance it is, the lead-manager should also deal with these problems as time permits. In all of these situations the manager must counsel, so learning to do this should be part of the preparation for lead-managing.

Once lead-managers develop a reputation for being capable of helping workers solve problems, the workers, having rarely been treated this well before at work, will increasingly bring problems to them. They will, however, realize that managers are not professional counselors and won't expect miracles. If all they do is lend sympathetic ears, workers will appreciate their effort and mark them as managers well worth working hard for.

In this brief chapter, I cannot teach counseling, but I can give some examples of the kinds of problems that managers are called upon to deal with, information that should prove helpful in many work situations. To develop counseling skills, it is anticipated that you will need some training in this area. Any organization that takes the ideas in this book seriously will offer its managers training in the counseling skills they need.

After being bossed for years, many workers will be fearful of even admitting they have a problem, so initially the lead-manager has to develop ways to encourage workers to bring problems to him. To do this, the manager has to state clearly from the beginning that he is only offering to help, not trying to blame or punish. What I suggest is that managers augment the sign previously suggested in Chapter 9 and post the following, more comprehensive message in all departments:

> In any workplace problems arise. These may
> be between the management and workers, among
> the workers, or just individual difficulties. What-
> ever they may be, if they are not solved to the
> satisfaction of all parties, we will be less able to
> produce quality products or render quality ser-
> vices, and our success as a company will suffer.

We believe it is the managers' job to help solve these problems and we take this job seriously. We also believe that all problems can be solved without the use of threats or punishment from us or any of the parties involved. It is our goal to create a workplace where we care for each other and where you can be confident that we are doing all we can to make this a good place to work. Only if we do this, will the company prosper and everyone earn what we and they believe is a fair wage.

After this sign goes up, it would be wise for the manager to gather the workers together and discuss what this sign means. The workers will tend to be skeptical, but if the manager is seen as beginning to practice what this sign preaches, a great deal of this skepticism will soon melt away. Also this sign will give the workers some idea of what is now going on: the change from bossing to leading. People don't like mysteries, and lead-managers make it their business to be open and above board in all they do.

Suppose a worker is chronically late for work. The manager should approach the worker and tell him that he thinks this is exactly the kind of problem he was referring to when he posted the sign. He could tell the worker that this will be a test of whether or not this new noncoercive approach will work. The worker will probably interrupt with an excuse or a complaint about the company, because that is what bossed workers have always done to avoid blame or punishment.

In his own words and with some give and take that I cannot exactly simulate, the manager should say, "I am not interested in excuses or complaints. I am also not interested in docking your wages or threatening you with the loss of your job. All I am interested in is how I can help you get here on time. I believe if we talk for a few minutes, we can work this out. What do you suggest that we, each of us, both you and I, can do that will get you here on time?" From this beginning, the manager and the worker would then talk and try to solve the problem.

After they have worked out a reasonable plan, the manager should say, "It is important that we talk again in a few days to see if what we discussed is working. If you have solved the problem, I want to make sure I know how you did it and what I did that may have helped. The more I know about how we solved this, the more I will be able to help another person with the same problem. Also, I may want you to talk to another person with a similar problem and tell him how you solved it. Would you be willing to help me if that situation came up again?" What is intended here is to get workers involved in helping each other solve small problems before they get too large. To do this, the lead-manager shifts as many problems as possible to the workers themselves and acts as a teacher in this process.

This was an easy problem in that it would have been impossible for the worker to deny it existed. Other problems will not be so obvious. For example, you may be asked to deal with a worker who is a good producer but who is holding up production because he insists on doing more than he can physically or mentally accomplish. Here the lead-manager must employ the key counseling technique of asking the worker to evaluate his own work as follows: "There seems to be a bottleneck here and I want to see if we can fix it. There is no question in my mind that you are working very hard and what you are doing is good work. But I want to talk with you about what seems to be a hold-up and get your opinion on what needs to be done to solve it. I can't solve this problem without some input from you."

Basic to noncoercive problem solving is to elicit the opinion or the judgment of the workers involved as to what they think the problem is. There is no threat here, only a genuine attempt to get as much input as possible from those involved. This also opens the door for the manager to give his input as to what he thinks the problem is. If he gave it in the usual boss way, the worker would take it as criticism and resist. But if he asks the worker first and listens carefully to what he has to say, it is likely the worker will then listen to him.

In this example, the worker may say the people who give him the work are giving it to him in such poor condition that he needs a lot of time to fix it. He claims he could work faster if they were doing their job as they should. You might not agree, but you would not voice that disagreement. You could say he may be right, but it may take some time for them to get their work in better shape and the problem needs to be solved quicker than this can be done. You can then tell him you think he has too much to do and, until he can take care of the incoming work, you want him to train a helper. You are not blaming or criticizing; you are offering him help and he may be willing to accept it.

However, he may not be willing to do as you suggest and you may have to take a different tack, but the point is that you have opened up the problem to solution by getting him to begin to evaluate his part, as well as the parts of others, in solving it. It may take several more evaluations, but this is the noncoercive way to deal with problems.

The more success the manager has in creating the noncoercive, problem-solving environment just discussed, the more likely it is that workers will bring problems to the manager. This is always better than the manager bringing up the problems, but the manager should not hesitate to bring them up. There is no need to wait for the workers to bring them to his attention. Once workers become aware of the fact that the manager is capable of helping them solve problems, whether he digs them up or they present them to him, the more the workers will be open to solving problems themselves, which is the ultimate goal of lead-managing.

Whether we like it or not, everything that goes on in the workers' lives that might lead to unhappiness has a potentially detrimental effect on the quality of the work they do. A hotel worker who is criticized a lot both at home and at work might take out his resentment by choosing not to write down an order to put a roll-away into a guest's room. The twisted logic behind this low-quality effort might be, "No one does anything special for me. Why should I do anything special for anyone else?"

Managers can't do anything about the home lives of their workers, but if the lead-manager provides the kind of work environment described so far, very few workers will take out their resentment of an unhappy home situation at work. This is one of the big pluses of lead-management. Still, workers will have nonwork-related problems that may eventually have a detrimental effect on their work if they are not solved. You should be prepared to offer to counsel any worker with any problem as long as you feel comfortable dealing with that particular situation.

Most workers are used to talking about their problems, but they are not used to getting effective help with them. Most of the advice they get from friends and family reinforces what is usually their initial opinion: the problem is someone else's fault. They latch on quickly and strongly to that opinion—in fact, almost all of us do, because we do not want to take responsibility for what is not working out well in our lives. To take responsibility, we have to admit we may have done something foolish or wrong. We sense a loss of power and, in a boss-managed workplace, we risk punishment. No one wants to lose power or to be punished: it is too painful.

Workers with serious problems that are affecting the quality of their work rarely have anyone to turn to who knows how to counsel effectively. They tend not to want to go to a professional counselor, because to do so would be to admit inadequacy, which is the same as saying, "I am not as capable as I should be." Also they mistakenly see counselors as professionals who treat crazy people and they, correctly, do not see themselves as crazy. They also fear that if they go to a counselor, and a boss finds out about it, as he may if the company is paying for it, this will be held against them and they may lose something important such as a promotion. And to some extent this fear is rational. Unfortunately, all of this prevents people from getting the help they need.

Even if managers are trained in some counseling skills, they should still be taught only to counsel the people they manage as long as they feel they can offer help. They should be warned that if they feel uncomfortable they would be better off not to get involved. However, my work in reality therapy,[1] the method of counseling I teach, has shown us that most of the problems that come up in the workplace can be handled easily and quickly by managers with a small amount of training in the use of these concepts. Since workers with unsolved problems are a source of low-quality work, the payoff in increased quality for solving them will far outweigh the small amount of time and money it takes to prepare managers for this important job.

Assuming the workers trust the lead-manager, counseling workers who ask for help will usually be effective. The manager should make at least twenty to thirty minutes of uninterrupted time available and should ask the worker to explain the problem as best as he can. Be patient and don't interrupt while he is explaining what's bothering him. For example, the worker may complain that he does not have enough help to do the job that he is assigned to do; it is just too much work. You believe that he is not working efficiently; he is stuck in some old habits and needs to learn the new way of doing things. After he is finished explaining the problem, ask him if he can see any other solution besides getting more help. Tell him the budget is short and you are appealing to his ingenuity. You want him to figure out how to solve this problem without anyone else doing anything differently.

Suppose he says he'll try, but he does not think he can do it: there is too much work. Tell him you appreciate that it's difficult for him, but say, "I want to ask you a question. Haven't you made up your mind that you need help, and have you really spent much time thinking about how you could solve the problem with no more help than you have? I am not criticizing, just asking about what may be going on." He will have to think about it, and as long as you are not seen as criticizing or threatening, he may agree that he has not really considered any other solution except more help. Tell him you would like him to really consider solving the problem with no more assistance and you will be happy to help him with whatever he figures out.

I can't predict how this will work out, but you may have persuaded the employee to shift to what you want and away from what he has been thinking about. If he can accept your idea that there is not going to be more assistance, that he has to work this out, he has a good chance of solving the problem. You helped him shift gears, and if you are right—that he can do the job without more assistance—he will be open to your explaining the new ways to work that he has previously rejected.

As you can see, this is not very hard to do. It is all based on the control theory concept of teaching a new total behavior and is the planning phase of reality therapy. It is far different from what a boss would do in that you don't step in with threats or try to take over the problem and impose a solution that would antagonize the employee so much he would never consider what you suggest as viable and would sabotage it as much as he can to prove his point.

To repeat, I am not citing these examples to try to make you into a counselor. All I am trying to do is show what you could do if you were willing to learn some reality therapy counseling techniques. It is done with the hope that you will see it is something you could learn. The good part about this way to counsel is that there is almost no risk. Even if you get into a problem that you realize is over your head, just admit you are stumped and back away. As long as you do not promise any more than to try to help, it is unlikely you will do any harm.

Let's take a personal problem that may be bothering a worker who is obviously suffering and is not as effective as she was. She tells you that her husband has left her, she is stuck with a lot of bills and no support, and she is at her wit's end. Ask her what she has done, for example, has she consulted a lawyer? When she tells you she has done nothing, that she is so upset she can barely come to work, she has no money for a lawyer, and you are the only person she can turn to, you have to suggest something. Although she is normally a very good worker, she feels so alone and powerless that her work is not up to what it usually is.

If she says that all she wants is for him to come back but that he won't even talk to her, suggest that the best thing she can do for the time being is to try to pull herself together, stop begging, and get along without him, since the reality is that she is without him anyway. Ask her, "What good does it do to try to get what seems impossible? In wanting what you can't get, aren't you just choosing to suffer? How does that help you? Neither of us can predict the future, but if you take my advice and he sees that you don't seem to need him, isn't he more likely to come back than if you run after him?"

Discuss this with her until she understands that strength far more than weakness is what attracts people and that your job is to help her to get stronger. Make sure to tell her that she is very appreciated at work, but she has to try to do a good job if she wants to feel good about herself. Tell her you want her to feel good at work and you sympathize with all she is going through. And you understand that coming to you shows she is serious about trying to solve the problem, which will be good for her both at home and at work.

You can't do much more than be supportive and give her a listening ear, but you can go out of your way to continue to tell her that (if this is indeed the case) even in her upset she still is doing fairly well at work. You might ask around and find a woman (not a man) at work who has gone through this experience successfully and get them together to talk. A person who has succeeded at anything that is hard to do is usually more than willing to help another person who is going through the same thing; this is very satisfying to that person's need for power. If you could put the worker in touch with legal aid, that would also be helpful.

With many of the people you help, it is not so much that you can do something specific as you can help them appreciate that no matter how bleak things seem, they can help themselves and, by being there, you give them the strength to try. Even if you don't do much, what I suggest here is usually so much more than they have available to them; what seems little to you is a great deal to them.

Finally, let's look at a more difficult problem. You know that a key worker is drinking off the job and, maybe, also a little at work, but he is too clever for you to catch him and I advise you not to try. If you catch him, you may have to be coercive or threatening, which would be counterproductive. If you are pretty sure of the facts, and you usually are, you need to confront him with the problem; how you do this is crucial. You should be very firm but as noncoercive as you can be. With an alcohol problem there may be no alternative to being somewhat coercive, but be very matter-of-fact, as if there is nothing else you can do except confront him with his drinking. You will come across as confrontive, which you are, but not very coercive, and this is about the best you can do with drinkers.

Tell him you believe he has a drinking problem and it is causing his work to suffer. If he denies it, as he likely will, tell him you expected he would deny it, but his denial is not going to make you change your mind. Explain that from your knowledge of drinking he has to stop or his work will deteriorate further, and he will not be able to stop unless he gets involved with a group like AA that has a good record of helping people like him stop drinking. Tell him he has to stop completely; there is all kinds of evidence to show that cutting down is impossible. Finally, tell him you are willing to do all you can to help, but there is not too much more you can do. It is up to him to take the first step and visit a program. The local alcohol foundation has lists of places where he can seek help. You should get a copy of this list and give it to him.

Tell him you want to talk with him tomorrow, but today, even if it is in the middle of a shift, he should go home. This way he knows you are serious. You will not have anyone you are managing remain at work if there is even a slight possibility of impairment. Tell him to come in early tomorrow to see you and tell you his plan. If your company and union rules allow, tell him he will not be allowed to go back to work until he has written and signed a plan, and it must start tomorrow, no later. If he says you are too hard, that you have no proof he even has a drinking problem, say this is all you will do. Anything less will not work and you care too much about him and his capacity to do a good job to do anything else.

You will, however, listen to him tomorrow even though you know he won't be able to come up with anything better, because what you are offering him is all there is. Addiction is a special problem that does not lend itself to counseling until the addict has actually stopped using the alcohol or other drugs. If you are not firm, he has little chance to regain control of his life. Once he is involved in a good plan, don't say anything more about his drinking. Any conversation about drinking and drugs is usually counterproductive in that he may see the discussion as vacillation on your part, think you are not really serious, and use this as an excuse to drink again. Don't fall into this trap.

Any manager who wants to learn to counsel as suggested in this chapter needs to do more than read this book. For further information on how to learn more about everything in this book, contact the Institute for Reality Therapy.[2]

Summing It Up

If you look around, you can't help but see that low quality pervades every part of our society. It must be replaced with quality or we will fade away to the level of a third world country. Much of what the government has done that makes achieving quality so difficult, such as tax breaks for hostile takeovers that lead to the looting and destruction of good companies and free markets to all no matter how they treat their workers, is well known but is not in my specific area of expertise. What I do know is that if we do not improve the way we manage the people who do the work in both profit and nonprofit organizations, working on other needed changes will be ineffective. All the large companies that are failing are in trouble because their employees were not managed to do the quality work I have taken pains to describe in this book.

We have to stop addressing the results of all the job losses such as moaning about the deficit and pay attention to the main way we can reduce it: more tax revenue

119

from more high-paying jobs in the private sector. The only way we will get these jobs is if we once again produce the finest products and services in the world. Not just a little better but significantly better and less costly than what others are able to produce. *We will be able to do this only if managers make the effort to conceptualize a quality workplace and then put that conception into their quality world. That is the first and continuing task of a control theory manager.*

We need to stop posturing and wallowing in self-delusion. We are not a great country as we enter the twenty-first century. We are sliding downhill into a sea of distrust and drowning in the lip service we give to ethics and morals, which mean little to people who are out of work. The ethics and morals that most people embrace stem from trust, hard work, and the achievement of quality. There is no shortcut to that truth.

Notes

CHAPTER ONE

1. W. Edwards Deming is the American who, starting in 1950, taught the Japanese a great deal about managing workers so that they do quality work. He is best known for his fourteen points or obligations of management. Except when otherwise stated, when I refer to his work in this book, my reference is: *A Day with Dr. Deming,* published by the Office of Naval Operations, Total Quality Leadership (OP-09BQ), The Pentagon Room 4E522, Washington, DC 20350-2000.

2. There is a more modern, scientific, stimulus-response psychology developed by B. F. Skinner that is much closer to control theory. This psychology explains that the response to the stimulus depends on whether the stimulus reinforces something operant in the organism. There is some doubt as to whether this could be called the completely intrinsic psychology that Deming advocates. It also does not accept the much more intrinsic control theory concepts such as basic genetic needs and the quality world and fails to explain the concept of total behavior. It has never gained popular

acceptance and has not replaced the popular S-R psychology that the public tends to follow.

3. Andrea Gabor, *The Man Who Brought Quality to America,* Random House, New York, 1990.

CHAPTER TWO

1. A good review of the research on what is essentially lead-management (he calls it "system four") is included in Rensis Likert, *Past and Future Perspectives on System 4,* 1977. This paper can be obtained from Rensis Likert Association, Inc., 630 City Center Building, Ann Arbor, MI 48104.

CHAPTER THREE

1. William Glasser, *The Quality School: Managing Students Without Coercion,* HarperCollins, New York, 1990.

2. The word *persuade* does not in any way imply that the manager uses any coercion. It is based on trust and the fact that the manager tries to convince the workers that to accept the manager's agenda will be beneficial to the workers as well as to the company.

CHAPTER FIVE

1. William Powers, *Behavior: The Control of Perception,* Aldine Press, Chicago, IL, 1973.

2. William Glasser, *Control Theory,* Harper & Row, New York, 1984.

3. TQM stands for total quality management, which usually means managing according to the ideas of Deming and other quality management experts.

4. From Lloyd Dobbins and Clare Crawford Mason, *Quality or Else,* Houghton Mifflin, Boston, MA, 1991.

5. There is no better description of the benefits of superb leadership in business than in the book written by the CEO of the highly successful and wonderfully human Herman Miller, Inc.: Max Depree, *Leadership Is an Art,* Dell, New York, 1989.

INTRODUCTION TO PART THREE
1. Dave Barry, *Dave Barry Does Japan,* Random House, New York, 1992.

CHAPTER ELEVEN
1. For more information, refer to: William Glasser, *Reality Therapy,* Harper & Row, New York, 1965.

2. Institute for Reality Therapy, 7301 Medical Center Drive, Suite 104, Canoga Park, CA 91307.